T0159148

Being
Lutheran
Today

A Layperson's Guide to Our History, Belief and Practice

The Rev. Dr. Derald H. Edwards
The Rev. Carsten J. Ludder

authorHOUSE®

AuthorHouse™
1663 Liberty Drive
Bloomington, IN 47403
www.authorhouse.com
Phone: 1 (800) 839-8640

© 2018 The Rev. Dr. Derald H. Edwards The Rev. Carsten J. Ludder. All rights reserved.

No part of this book may be reproduced, stored in a retrieval system, or transmitted by any means without the written permission of the author.

Published by AuthorHouse 08/22/2018

ISBN: 978-1-5462-3515-6 (sc)
ISBN: 978-1-5462-3514-9 (e)

Library of Congress Control Number: 2018903679

Print information available on the last page.

Any people depicted in stock imagery provided by Getty Images are models, and such images are being used for illustrative purposes only. Certain stock imagery © Getty Images.

This book is printed on acid-free paper.

Because of the dynamic nature of the Internet, any web addresses or links contained in this book may have changed since publication and may no longer be valid. The views expressed in this work are solely those of the author and do not necessarily reflect the views of the publisher, and the publisher hereby disclaims any responsibility for them.

[Scripture quotations are] are from the Revised Standard Version of the Bible, copyright © 1946, 1952, and 1971 the Division of Christian Education of the National Council of the Churches of Christ in the United States of America. Used by permission. All rights reserved.

ACKNOWLEDGEMENTS

In remembrance of the 500th year anniversary of the Reformation

In honor of Charlsie Doolittle for her encouragement to write this book, and whose painstaking time was given so graciously to read, re-read, and edit the contents of this resource throughout the project.

In honor of Chris Brooks for her encouragement to write this book, and who spent an enormous amount of hours typing the manuscript and researching the artistic headings and images used throughout each chapter.

A special thanks to Pomaria Lutheran Church for your patience in seeing this project through.

8 Reasons Why You Should Use this Resource

Over the years, the following questions have been posed to all Lutheran pastors.

1. What is a Lutheran? It is amazing that this question is still asked as we celebrate the 500th anniversary of the Lutheran Church in the year 2017.
2. Isn't the Lutheran Church just like the Roman Catholic Church? And the answer is NO, it is no more Roman Catholic than any other Protestant denomination. It is simply that we are a liturgical Protestant Church.
3. Do Lutherans worship Martin Luther? The answer is that Lutherans worship only God in Jesus Christ. Luther is just held in high regard.
4. Where should one begin when reading the Bible? The answer comes from the fact that you must first begin with knowledge about Jesus Christ. Therefore, the first place to seek that is in the book of Mark. When finished with Mark, then go to the book of Luke, then Matthew, and then John.
5. How does one becomes a Christian? The answer to that takes place in the sacrament of Holy Baptism. Baptism unites us with the risen Christ and makes us members of God's family.
6. Isn't Holy Communion simply a memorial? The answer is, once again, no. The Scriptures proclaim that in Holy Communion one receives the body and blood of Jesus Christ through bread and wine.
7. Why is worship in the Lutheran church sometimes misunderstood by those looking from the outside in. We are a liturgical church which requires an ordered pattern of worship where all participate equally at the same time. It is something you do, not something you merely observe. Liturgy means "the work of the people."
8. What is the Apostles creed? The Apostles creed is an expression of the one holy, catholic, and apostolic faith. In this creed we acknowledge the triune God, and while the word Trinity is not

mentioned in the Bible, the formula is there thus revealing to us that God is Three in One.

These and a myriad of other questions that come to people's hearts and minds can be answered by reading this resource. In doing so, you will have a greater understanding of the history, belief and practice of the Lutheran church.

The Rev. Dr. Derald H. Edwards   The Rev. Carsten J. Ludder

FOREWORD

Once, during a clergy group meeting, I was complaining about the lack of good teaching tools and how I invariably found myself writing material rather than using off-the-shelf products. It was during one such time that my friend and colleague Derald Edwards invited me to use this book as a teaching tool.

I have known The Reverend Dr. Derald Edwards for many years and know him to be a man of God with a love of learning and teaching. He embraces and engages the power of the Holy Spirit in all that he does – whether preaching a sermon, visiting a shut in, or talking with a friend. His passion for the work he is called to do is infectious.

Each year of my ministry, I am tasked with reaching children, youth, and adults in novel ways to help them understand the faith into which we are baptized. This understanding is something that one can acquire from years of worship, Sunday school, and Bible study, but is something from which many still find themselves disconnected. Many regular church goers find it difficult to explain what exactly it means to be a Lutheran. And some youth successfully complete the confirmation process but come back to me years later, still unsure of how to articulate and stand up for their faith. It can often be difficult to offer answers in a clear and concise way. But regardless of where people are in their faith formation and understanding of being Lutheran, Derald Edwards and Carsten Ludder have created in their new book *Being Lutheran Today: A Layperson's Guide to our History, Belief and Practice,* the most effective catechism tool I have used in recent years.

This book is a very helpful resource for those congregations seeking to reach out to previously un-churched members or members transferring from different denominations. Our congregation used this book during the Season of Lent as a tool in both our adult and high school Sunday school classes. In addition to being an effective resource in developing an understanding of the Lutheran faith, this book also acts as a welcome refresher on the fullness of our faith and practices, successfully reaching out to members of all backgrounds and understandings.

The easy-to-read format and easy-to-understand writing style of this book makes it particularly enjoyable to read and share with others. It begins by giving the reader a history of the subject, and each successive chapter digs deeper into the faith practices of Lutherans, allowing the reader to develop a thorough understanding of the material. I encourage Christian education leaders, pastors, and anyone wanting to understand who we are as a denomination to read this fantastic book and learn about our heritage and practices as Lutherans.

The Rev. Patti Sue Burton-Pye
Providence Lutheran Church
Lexington, South Carolina

CONTENTS

FAITH: Hebrews 11:1
"Now faith is the substance of things hoped for, the evidence of things not seen."
HOPE: Luke 24:5-6
"Why do you look for the living among the dead?
He is not here, but has been raised."
LOVE: I Corinthians 13:13
"And now these three remain: faith, hope, and
love. But the greatest of these is love."

A familiar combination of emblems is a cross, an empty tomb and a heart.
These signify FAITH, HOPE and LOVE.

CHAPTER 1

A Short History of Lutheranism

To understand how the Reformation could have happened in the first place, we first need to understand the condition of society on the eve of the Reformation. The Reformation couldn't have happened if the atmosphere wasn't just right. Conditions in the world at the time were what led up to this tremendous explosion, not only in the church, but in society as well.

The world before the Reformation seemed much smaller. Prior to that time, the world was immensely undiscovered and unknown. However, that began to change in the fifteenth century. Within the span of fifty or so years, such explorers as Henry the Navigator, Diaz, De Gama, Columbus and Magellan had sailed forth from their respective countries and were discovering vast new lands. It was a time of expansion and excitement.

With the birth of this new era came not only the discovery of the world but also the vast reaches of the universe. Nicolaus Copernicus, a Polish astronomer, put forth an amazing theory stating that the earth was just one of many marvelous bodies in the solar system. He believed these bodies seemed to be revolving around the sun which rested near the center of the universe and that the earth revolved on its axis once a day and revolved once a year around the sun. It later became known as the heliocentric or sun-centered system. Theologically speaking then, his theory rejected the long held belief concerning a three-tier universe: that heaven was above, hell was below and the earth lay in between the two.

Then came the breakdown of the economic system of feudalism, giving rise to nationalism. This was generally the idea that individual territories were to be protected, as were the interests of groups of people within them.

At the same time, there was also a rebirth of art and literature in the era of Michelangelo, Raphael, da Vinci, and many other artistic masters. With the fall of Constantinople to the Turks in 1453, many scholars bolted to Italy with the manuscripts of the Greek masters, who challenged people to discover truth and beauty above all else. So, it was a time of intellectual awakening and a time of discovery.

It was during this time the printing press was invented. Moveable-type become quicker than wood-block printing. This was possibly the chief single accomplishment the world knew at that time. With this accomplishment came the opportunity for accepted wisdom and material to be disseminated and distributed across the known world. The opportunity for education, which until then was only for the privileged few, now became possible for all. The common folk no longer had to depend on the clergy to inform them about what the Bible said; they could for the first time begin to read and understand it as Luther begin translating the scriptures in German, the language of the people. The old certainties were breaking down. Society was taking the next step forward as well, an awakening that would grow to become a tool of the reformers.

Everything was stirring everywhere. Everywhere, that is, except in the church. There, the old ways perpetuated, for the church's authority and power were absolute. People were taught and believed that salvation was a risky thing at best and one's only avenue to salvation was through the church. It would be very difficult today to imagine the tremendous grip the Pope had on the people. With one word he could assign anyone to eternal damnation. This power was handed down to the local priest without whose services you could not be saved.

If you weren't baptized, you couldn't be saved and only the church could baptize. If you didn't go to confession, you couldn't be saved, and only the church could hear confession. In a very real way, the church held the keys to the gates of heaven. The church has always had its dark times and dark leaders but the main problem leading up to the Reformation was the church's insistence on being more political than religious.

Among the protestant churches in the world, the Lutheran Church is both the oldest and one of the largest. It was founded upon Jesus Christ and carried on by his faithful followers today. It is a true expression of the one true Holy catholic and apostolic church. The disciples, known later as apostles, were the first to lead the early church after Christ's resurrection and they shared Christ's teaching with all whom they encountered. It was in house churches that early Christians worshiped and shared the gospel. These Christians gathered together in the home of the followers, often secretly, due to the religious political climate of the day.

It was in this environment that the Reformation movement of the 1500s and the Lutheran tradition had its beginnings. It was led by a Roman Catholic monk named Martin Luther who was born in Eisleben, Germany in 1483. Luther was the son of a copper miner. Martin's home was generally a happy one, but his parents, Hans and Margaret Luther, were very strict disciplinarians. Hans and Margaret were devout Catholics. Unfortunately, Martin was raised with an image of Jesus as a severe judge who would willingly punish Christians, were it not for the intersession of his mother, Mary, and John the Baptist.

Luther, a brilliant student of theology and scripture, became a monk against the desires of his father who wished his son to become a lawyer. He was ordained as a priest at the age of 23 in 1507. Five years later, Luther earned his doctorate in theology and was appointed a Professor of Theology at the University of Wittenberg. After years of exhaustive Bible study, Luther became torn between devotion to the Roman Catholic Church and his own conscience criticizing some of the churches most basic teachings. Luther came to believe intensely that salvation was a precious gift from God alone to those who had faith in Jesus Christ – not achieved by so-called good works or through councils, priests or clerical mediators. This became known as the doctrine of "justification by grace, received through faith."

Troubled by his own innermost turmoil and convictions, Luther, from what he read and discovered and knew in the scriptures, began stressing three important teachings: justification by grace through faith; the universal priesthood of all believers; and the supremacy of scripture. All this he formulated from his intensive reading of the Bible.

Luther also begin to question the Roman Catholic Church's practice of selling *indulgences,* a main complaint of his, a practice that had developed over a period of many years. About 1000 years before, if someone was guilty of some serious sin, he or she was cut off from the church. In order to be reinstated, one had to make confession and perform some good work or satisfaction to make up for the error. Fasting or a pilgrimage, for instance, might be required of that person. But the Pope made it possible for those in too poor of health to perform such works to give money instead. This money would be seen as the good work of almsgiving.

This eventually gave rise to the concept of the Treasury of Merit which said that Jesus and his disciples had lived such good lives that they had built up an inexhaustible supply of merit. The Pope could, at his discretion, assign this merit to sinners if they didn't have enough of their own. But this merit wasn't just given away. It had to be purchased in the form of an indulgence, which was a piece of paper allowing so much forgiveness—or merit—for so much money (a good work of almsgiving). No longer did one have to be sorry for his/her sin. Forgiveness from God was now a business transaction for which one paid. It could even be bought in advance if you contemplated some future sin. You could also buy indulgences for the dead in purgatory to lessen the duration of their stay there. It was this practice that got Luther hopping mad. He said an indulgence "is of no value at all, except to fan yourself in hell."

In 1517, Luther began formulating his disputation against scholastic theology and nailed his famous *Ninety-five Theses* to the door of the

Castle Church in Wittenberg, Germany. His intention, by making these theses public, was to invite serious discussion among scholars, priests, and all concerned. No one accepted the invitation, but the *Ninety-five Theses* were copied, printed, and sent around the empire and to other universities. Within a matter of weeks, Luther's name was well known. Finally, there was someone with the determination and courage to voice his opinion against the shameful condition of the church.

Luther's posting of the *Ninety-five Theses* angered the Pope and leading church leaders of the day. They commanded Luther to appear in Rome to answer charges of heresy. However, Elector Frederick the Wise of Saxony intervened and pleaded for Luther's hearing to be held on German territory. So, in October of 1518, a hearing known as the Diet of Augsburg was held at Augsburg, Germany. Upon being examined by the Papal representative, Cardinal Cajetan, Luther refused to renounce his views. Fearing he might be detained and whisked off to Rome, Luther fled. Prince Fredrick, being well respected by the Pope, gave Luther the opportunity to debate his views publicly. His opponent was the famous scholar and theologian of the day, Jon Eck.

Eric Gritsch and Robert Jenson state:

> On November 18, 1518, Luther solemnly appealed to Pope Leo X to call a general ecumenical council to debate the reform of the Roman Catholic Church. In the presence of a notary and two witnesses in the Wittenberg Corpus Christi Chapel, he declared in a carefully drafted statement: 'I do so with the expressed and solemn assurance that I shall do nothing against the one, holy, catholic church, which I regard as the master of the entire world, and thus as supreme, or against the prestige of the holy apostolic see, or against our most Holy Lord, the Pope, if he is well informed. If, however, I should utter something that is not right or is said with irreverence, prompted by my opponents, I am quite willing to correct and to change it.[1]

Luther contended that the papacy was a human institution not of divine origin, which swiftly got him into trouble. When Luther and Eck debated the primacy of the papacy at Leipzig in 1519, Luther advanced the understanding that the church of Christ extends far beyond the narrow confines of the Roman Church. "I brought up the Greek Christians of the past thousand years," he told his friend George Spalatin shortly after the debate, "and also the ancient fathers who had not been under the authority of the Roman pontiff, although I did not deny the primacy of honor due to the pope." (LW 31, 322) Subsequent experience taught Luther that such pleas to a council or authority were of no help.

Paul Althaus, in his book *The Theology of Martin Luther*, says:

> Luther recognizes the Holy Spirit has been promised to the church of Christ. But this is not necessarily promised to the gathering of the bishops or the council. This means that no council can cite the promise of the Holy Spirit to prove its decrees and drive binding authority for its canons from this promise of the Holy Spirit. The ecclesiastical legitimacy of such a gathering does not necessarily include its spiritual legitimacy. This later depends completely on the apostolicity of its doctrines and resolutions. It hardly seems necessary to mention that Luther would say the same about the claim of the highest teaching office of the church. The First Vatican Council's dogma that the Pope's teaching ex cathedra is infallible is subject to the same criticism as the dogma that the council is infallible.[2]

Luther's ideas concerning reform quickly spread. The pope refuted Luther's view with a Papal Bull (order), threatening Luther with excommunication from the church unless he renounced his beliefs. He had sixty days to respond. Luther published his answer to the Papal Bull which threatened him with excommunication. Luther responded by holding a public gathering in Wittenberg and burned the Papal Bull before the crowed.

With Luther's refusal to retract his words, the Imperial Diet of Worms issued the Edict of Worms declaring Luther an outlaw which carried the sentence of capital punishment. Fortunately for Luther, Emperor Charles V had promised Luther safe passage to and from the Diet of Worms upon his attendance. On his return to Wittenberg, Luther was kidnapped by Elector Frederick of Saxony, the ruler of the region in which Wittenberg University was located. It was a friendly kidnapping, however, in that Luther had become a national folk hero that put Wittenberg University, an institution highly prized by Fredrick, on the map. Everyone was looking to Wittenberg and Luther for the new social ethic, the new society, the new church! Therefore, Frederick ignored the Edict of Worms and gave Luther safe haven in the Wartburg Castle.

While in hiding, Luther sought to reform Christian doctrine and practice. Recognizing the Bible as God's word and the true source of doctrine, he believed the Word of God received in faith and revealed as the Holy Gospel was the true way to salvation, and that no one had to go through council, priest, or pope to get to God. This knowledge later became known as the "priesthood of all believers." His reforms also included the knowledge that Holy Baptism and the Lord's Supper were the only true sacraments of the church rather than the seven that were recognized by the church of his day.

In his treatise "The Babylonian Captivity," Luther took issue with the seven sacraments of the Roman Catholic Church in light of his understanding of the Bible. With regard to Holy Communion, he demanded that the cup reserved only for the priest be restored to the laity. He insisted that the Catholic belief in transubstantiation be rejected, but affirms the real presence of the body and blood of Christ is "in, with, and under" the bread and wine in the Eucharist meal. He also rejected the teaching that Mass is a sacrifice offered over and over to God each time communion is celebrated. Luther writes that baptism brings justification only if it is joined with saving faith in one who receives it; however, it remains the foundation of one's salvation, even for those who might later reject the faith but then be restored.

Paul Althus says:

> Luther felt that a sacrament consists in the combination of the word of promise with a sign, that is, it is a promise accompanied by a sign instituted by God, and a sign accompanied by a promise. This means, first, that a sign or a symbol by itself is not yet a sacrament. Luther explains that every visible act can naturally mean something and be understood as a picture of an analogy of invisible realities, but that is not enough however, to make a symbolic act into a sacrament. The symbolic act must be instituted or commanded by God, combined with a promise.[3]

In his book *Wishful Thinking, A Seeker's ABC*, Frederick Buechner offers a different perspective in his modern and delightful description of a sacrament:

> A sacrament is when something holy happens. It is transparent time, time which you can see through to something deep inside time. Generally speaking, Protestants have two official sacraments (Baptism and the Lord's Supper) and Roman Catholic's these two and five others, (Confirmation, penance, Extreme Unction, Ordination, and Matrimony) In other words, at such milestone moments as seeing a baby baptized or being baptized yourself, confessing your sins getting married, dying, you are apt to catch a glimpse of the almost unbearable preciousness and mystery of life. Needless to say, church isn't the only place where the holy happens. Sacramental moments can occur at any moment, any place, and to anybody. Watching something get born. Making love. A walk on the beach. Somebody coming to see you when you're sick. A meal with people you love. Looking into a stranger's eyes and finding out he's not a stranger. If we weren't blind as bats, we might see that life itself is sacramental.[4]

In 1526, Luther produced a vernacular liturgy called the German Mass for which he sought to give worship back to the people. He also asserted that both laity and clergy should partake of the wine as well as the bread within the setting of the Mass. Before 1526, the wine was reserved only for the priest, but withheld from the laity.

Luther believed that the individual conscience is answerable only to the Word of God. Christ alone, he taught, is the intermediary between humanity and the creator, not a council, not the priest, nor the pope. Baptism makes all member of "the priesthood of all believers."

The Reform movement grew quickly in the years following Luther's clash with the church. More and more people accepted and believed Luther's teachings and those of other reformation leaders. Various groups broke away from the Roman Catholic Church. The 1500s were a time of political upheaval. German princes sought to distinguish themselves from the Holy Roman Empire and demanded to rule their territories for the privilege of being protestant or Roman Catholic as they dictated. Disgruntled peasants began to organize and stood up to the feudalism under which they were suffering. As a result, changes in Christian doctrine became widely accepted in Germany's atmosphere of swift social.

By 1526, Catholic masses (worship services) were being celebrated in German rather than Latin; countless German territories had established their own churches apart from Rome. The reformers began being called Protestants when they protested theological rulings made by the Diet of Speyer in 1529.

In an attempt to reach a compromise, Roman Catholic and Protestant leaders met at Augsburg in 1530. Philip Melanchthon, Luther's close friend, fellow theologian, and the author of the *Augsburg Confession,* sought to explain Luther's position, attempting to reconcile Catholic and Protestant beliefs. Three basic doctrines of the Lutheran understanding of scripture were outlined. They are 1) Justification by faith alone - Sola Fide; 2) Salvation through grace alone - Sola Gratia; and 3) Doctrine from scripture alone - Sola Scripture. Therefore the reformers cry became faith over works;

grace over merit; and scripture over tradition, each intentionally stated to represent chief differences compared with Roman Catholic doctrine. This *Augsburg Confession* later became one of the official doctrinal statements of the Lutheran Church, as it remains today.

Finally, in the year 1555, after much sparring among the Roman Catholics and Protestants, the Peace of Augsburg was signed. Hostilities against others on religious grounds would no longer be tolerated. Each German territory was granted permission to determine whether it would be Catholic or Protestant, depending on the ruling prince's religion. Subjects were free to move to territories where their religion was practiced. People living in large cities where both religions were practiced would have the opportunity to worship as they wished.

It was through rough, dangerous, and agonizing times that lives were lost over religious beliefs. Lutheran Protestants, seeking to resolve doctrinal disputes and make clear their own beliefs published the *Book of Concord* in 1580, which remains the foundation for Lutherans to this day.

The end of the 1500s saw Lutheranism becoming the recognized church in all Scandinavian countries. It gained extensive influence in other countries as well. In the early 1600s, Lutheran beliefs and theology expanded to the new world, and great and dedicated missionary efforts spread it over much of the globe.

In the 1850s, many new immigrants came to America, scores of them Lutheran. These new immigrants joined other Lutherans in establishing numerous sovereign territorial regions called synods. These were commonly organized around cultural and ethnic heritage within geographical settings. With such diverse ethnic groups, many of which had Lutheran backgrounds, there was a sense of natural divisions. Therefore, early attempts were made to combine Lutheran groups divided by language, culture, and doctrine. Some of these early attempts included 1) The General Synod of 1820; 2) the General Council of 13 Synods, 1867; 3) The Synodical Conference of Midwestern Churches of 1872; and 4) the United Synod South of 1866.

In 1888, the Common Service Hymnal was published by several synods and was used extensively by all American Lutherans of that time period.

Throughout the twentieth century, progress toward church unity developed. However, unity and diversity, splits and pullouts continue to occur even today. In 1988 the Evangelical Lutheran Church was formed, which included the Lutheran Church in America, the Association of Evangelical Lutheran Churches, and the American Lutheran Church. The Lutheran Church Missouri Synod refused to join due to doctrinal differences. The latest major change occurred in 2010, when members of the Evangelical Lutheran Church of America (ELCA) pulled out to form the North American Lutheran Church (NALC). The NALC officially formed in 2010 from congregations, laypeople, and clergy that broke away from the ELCA (and of Canada) over issues of scriptural authority. The crisis point came following the ELCA's 2009 decision to bless same-sex relationships and allow noncelibate homosexual people to be ordained.

As one of the largest Protestant denominations, the ELCA belongs to the Lutheran World Federation, which serves as a worldwide Lutheran organization. While divisions continue to occur in the Lutheran Church, the faithful seek to remain true to the gospel and to proclaim the Word of God in purity and doctrine through loving service to others. She also strives for Christian unity while maintaining a Lutheran identity.

In summary, Lutherans share a rich heritage. A Lutheran is first and foremost a Christian, and Christians trust in Jesus Christ as Savior. Lutherans are sinners but are forgiven. Lutherans share a common faith with other Christians. We accept the Bible as the true source of Christian love, guidance, and doctrine. We accept the ancient creeds of the church: the Apostles, Nicene, and Athanasius Creeds. We are diligent in the use of the means of grace, preaching of the gospel and administering the sacraments of baptism and the Lord's Supper.

Lutherans understand the *Book of Concord* to be their testimony as the correct and true interpretation of God's Holy Word, written to correct church errors. It contains five major parts: 1) the Augsburg Confession; 2) the Apology of the Augsburg Confession; 3) the Smalcald Articles; 4) the Formula of Concord; and 5) Luther's Small and Large Catechisms.

Lutherans proclaim God's message by emphasizing justification by faith through grace. We teach that the Bible is not a book of dos and don'ts, but a book telling about the love of God in Jesus Christ and all that means for our lives. We are people who are freed from the law and free to love others and God according to His way and will. The Lutheran church then, is part of the one holy catholic (universal) church and the apostolic faith, a means through which the Holy Spirit works to help Christians grow in grace. We are congregational, but do not limit our activities to local and regional arenas. We are a confessional church that acknowledges Jesus as Lord and the Bible as the inspired word of God that reveals God's will for our lives. We are an ecumenical church that works for the unity of all Christians everywhere. We are a visible church where we gather to hear God's word and receive the sacraments. We are part of the invisible church that Jesus founded upon his resurrection, made up of all who believe they are saved through faith in him.

NOTES

CHAPTER 2

What It Means to Be a Lutheran

The Lutheran church was forged in the fire of controversy during the Reformation as it could no longer abide by the teachings and practices of the Roman Church. This controversy not only led the Lutherans to articulate what they didn't believe, but also to defend what they did. And in a series of writings that took place between 1529 and 1577, our church set down for the ages its faith and practice.

These are what are known as our confessional documents. They are contained in a collection of works called the "Formula of Concord." When we say that the Lutheran Church is a confessional church, we mean to say that we have a stated body of belief, which we use to guide and test the faith and practice of our church.

Lutherans have always had a very strong self-identity. Our faith and our practice are solidly rooted in the scriptures and our confessions. Therefore, we are, ecumenically speaking, an easy church to dialogue with because our position is always relatively clear in that other denominations can read our book as well as we can. We think that self-knowledge is a strength. Basic premises keep us from drifting about with every wind of doctrine. Below are set forth some of the basics on which Lutherans stand.

Today, there are some 50 million Lutherans worldwide. We are the first, the oldest, and one of the largest Protestant denominations in the world.

However, Lutherans do not believe that they are the only true church. We maintain that the true church is invisible and cuts across all denominational lines.

Those who are joined together through water and the word, or said another way, through baptism and the preaching and hearing of the gospel, belong to the church of Jesus Christ. This is why Lutherans maintain an open stance ecumenically.

Martin Luther was historically the first Lutheran, a Roman Catholic monk who tried to cure some abuses by the Roman Church during the sixteenth century. However, he never wanted the church to call itself by his name.

Actually, Luther felt that the term "evangelical" was best because it means we preach the good news of Christ. The official name of most Lutheran churches does include the name evangelical. The official name of our greater church, for example, is the Evangelical Lutheran Church in America.

In the past, Lutherans have been accused of worshiping Luther, but that is not true. We worship only God in Jesus Christ. Luther is simply held in high regard.

As a monk, Luther naturally kept many of the traditions of the Catholic Church and discarded only those which he considered, on the basis of Scripture, improper or harmful. Thus, Lutheran churches have a central altar symbolizing the place where we meet Christ, two candles symbolizing the human and divine natures of Christ, and an adorned cross (i.e. a cross that has upon it some representation of Christ because our focus should never be on the cross per se, but rather on the man who died on the cross for the salvation of humanity). Also, in a liturgical worship space, the cross is put in a place of central focus. In addition, we have a liturgical service, which follows an ordered pattern. Seasonal altar hangings, paraments, are displayed to signify the seasons or festival Sundays of the church year in a liturgical worship space. Lutheran church ministers are robed during the service.

All this has prompted some folks to ask: "Isn't the Lutheran Church just like the Catholic Church?" No, it is no more Catholic than any other protestant church. It is simply that we are A LITURGICAL PROTESTANT CHURCH.

The Lutheran liturgical service is not form and ceremony for its own sake. Every element has significance in the act of worship. In some sense, a liturgical worship service is like a play or re-enactment of the salvation story. Hundreds of years of experience has taught us that this form of service is best suited to give a broad expression to the worship of God. However, broad discretion is allowed in the form, content and music of a liturgical worship service.

In most Lutheran churches today, the pastor wears an alb, a white liturgical vestment, which symbolizes the purity of Christ. It is the oldest Christian vestment dating back to the sixth century. The stole simply serves as a reminder that the pastor has upon his or her shoulders the burden and yoke of Christ and is, therefore, a sign of ordination.

The Lutheran church is different from many other Protestant churches as it legislates on very few matters. Lutherans believe that it is not the use, but the abuse of things that constitutes intemperance. That is why the Lutheran church has never legislated, for instance, against alcohol or tobacco.

As a rule, Lutheran preachers (at least the good ones), rarely discuss political matters from the pulpit because they believe that the preaching of the gospel is not only more important, but also the true mandate and obligation of the church. We are an evangelical church. We are to be about proclaiming the good news of Christ. We believe that there is power in the gospel to make new men and women, and new men and women can and will remake the world.

Lutherans hold that Sunday is the Lords day, but do not hedge it about with all sorts of legalistic requirements. However, Lutherans do insist on worship on the Lord's day. To ask if someone can get to heaven without going to church is like asking if you can get to Europe without getting on an ocean liner or plane. Well, one could row or swim, but it isn't safe. Whoever believes in Jesus Christ and looks to receive his promise of eternal life will want to join the Christian Church.

In the Lutheran Church it is a fundamental principle that the scriptures are the supreme and only authority for matters of faith (what we believe) and life (what we practice). Also Lutherans do accept the Bible as the inspired word of God. Our belief in the inspiration of the Bible does not mean that God crossed every t and dotted every i in the King James Version of the Bible and dropped it down from heaven intact. Rather the constitution of the Evangelical Lutheran Church in America puts it this way:

"The canonical Scriptures of the Old and New Testament are the written word of God. Inspired by God's Spirit speaking through their authors, they record and announce God's revelation centering in Jesus Christ. Through them, God's Spirit speaks to us to create and sustain Christian faith and fellowship for service in the world."

Regarding conversion, Lutherans believe that everyone must be returned from sin to righteousness. We believe that sin - a turning against God and his will - is the basic condition of our hearts and is thus original sin. We are not sinners because we sin occasionally, but we sin occasionally because we are sinners.

Furthermore, we believe that this change or conversion from our sinful nature to God's righteousness or living more according to God's will is brought about by the operation of the Holy Spirit through the repeated hearing of the Word and receiving of the Sacrament. This is why faithful participation in the services of God's house is seen as most important.

Through the law, God brings about a knowledge of sin and sorrow for it. The Gospel reveals Jesus Christ as the savior from sin and the example of righteous living. It is said that Luther in his preaching hammered the people down with the law and then lifted them up to new life with the gospel.

Lutherans hold that everyone who is truly sorry for their sins and believes that Jesus Christ is their savior is converted. And we do not hold that conversion must necessarily take on a violent form or that the process in every case be a conscious experience. This is why Lutherans practice infant baptism.

Lutherans believe in baptism of both adults and infants. Our concept of baptism follows the tradition of St. Paul, which is being incorporated into the family of God. Just as a Jewish baby was incorporated into the tribe or family of God for life through circumcision, so a child is incorporated or made part of God's family forever in Holy Baptism.

For Lutherans, baptism is not a way by which we acknowledge our love for God, but a way by which God demonstrates his love of us. In infant baptism, God reaches into the life of a child through the parents and the church. Together they are entrusted to guide his or her Christian development until they reach the age of thirteen or so. At that time, they undergo a course of instruction in the Christian faith for up to three years, which is called Confirmation. After confirmation instruction, the child is confirmed as he or she vows loyalty to Christ as an adult member of the church.

So why do Lutherans baptize infants who are without faith or knowledge? First, because we want this child to be part of the family of God from the very beginning and because we feel that the seriousness of sin requires prompt action. We say that a child learns more in the first years of its life than any other. If that is true, then we want our children to be involved in the community of faith from the very beginning.

Some parents might say, "We don't want to force religion on our children. When they grow up, they can make up their own minds." For one thing, that is a cop out. That same reasoning wouldn't apply about school or going to the doctor. Should we not "force" education or health on our children and instead wait until they can make up their minds about it?

Additionally, not having infant baptism leads to generations of people being totally out of touch with the church and without the power of Jesus

Christ in their lives as well. If you were in a dangerous place and had an opportunity to escape, you wouldn't ask your infant daughter if she wanted to come with you? No! You would decide for her and thereby make a determination that would influence the rest of her life. That is exactly what we do for a child in infant baptism. The parents make a decision for them that will influence the rest of the child's life.

As a matter of convenience, Lutherans sprinkle in baptism for it is not the amount of water that is used in baptism that makes it valid, but rather the promises of God's Word together with the water.

Lutherans do not believe that the Lord's Supper is only a memorial meal for the remembrance of Christ, but that it offers something truly profound. It was instituted by Christ for the forgiveness of sins. It is a visible word demonstrating God's love for us. It is like a great big bear hug from God that shows us how much he loves us, that he forgives us, and that he is truly present with us always. It is an assurance to every believer that his or her sins have been forgiven and that they have a renewed fellowship with God.

So far, we have provided a brief overview of what we believe as Lutherans. However, the central question of the Reformation that led to the formation of the Lutheran Church was: "How are we saved?"

The Roman Catholic system in Luther's day was a system of earning or losing merit on earth which determined one's entry into heaven. Luther and the Reformers said that you were not saved by your works, but rather by your faith in Christ Jesus. The only mediator of salvation was Jesus and it was only through him that we could come to eternal life. Therefore, we are justified, or made right before God, or saved by grace alone through faith.

There are FIVE ALONES that are hallmarks of Lutheran theology:

FAITH ALONE: We are made right with God only through faith in Jesus Christ as Savior. Salvation is Christ's work through the cross mediated to us by faith.

19

GRACE ALONE: Grace is God's unmerited love, a love that is not dependent on our acts, but on God's determination. God loves us because he is the "500 pound gorilla" of love. It sits wherever it wants. This grace, or demonstration of God's love, awakens faith in us. Thus, we come to salvation by grace through faith.

Luther's explanation to the 3rd Article of the Apostles' Creed in his *Small Catechism* states, "I believe that I cannot by my own reason or strength believe in Jesus Christ, my Lord, or come to Him; but the Holy Spirit has called me through the Gospel, enlightened me with his gifts, sanctified and kept me in the true faith; even as he calls, gathers, enlightens, and sanctifies the whole Christian Church on earth..."

CHRIST ALONE: Jesus said, "I am the way, and the truth and the life. No one comes to the Father, except through me" (John 14:6). Jesus is the sole mediator with God between this life and the life to come.

SCRIPTURE ALONE: The Bible is the sole authority for our faith and our practice as Christians. We have no appeal to any other authority.

GLORY TO GOD ALONE: Our works as Christians do nothing to merit consideration before God. This is the place of faith alone. Therefore, our works of love and service are done for God's glory, not for ours.

NOTES

CHAPTER 3

A Short History of the Bible

While one might regard the Bible as a book, it is actually a library of books written by many different authors over a period of more than a thousand years. The word bible comes from the Konia Greek word *biblia,* which means books. The Bible is a collection of ancient and inspired writings about God and God's people. The Bible has two parts, the Old Testament and the New Testament scriptures. Testament means agreement or covenant and the word scripture means sacred writings. When we speak of the Genesis-to-Revelation gathered works described as the Bible, the individual books in this collection are assumed to be related to one another as parts of a larger union, i.e. one book. The term scripture (or Greek *graphe,* meaning written material) merely refers to biblical literature. In the broadest sense of the word, it means religious literature used in the life of a religious community.

The Protestant Church recognizes sixty-six writings or books as the Bible, thirty-nine in the Old Testament and twenty-seven in the New Testament. This is often denoted as the canon or accepted books. However, the Roman Catholic Church recognizes seventy-three writings or books as their canon. The seven books not included in the canon of the Protestant church are called the Apocrypha.

Christians believe inspired writers wrote these accepted books. God guided these inspired writers with the Holy Spirit, to understand His word correctly so they might communicate His message of salvation to all people for all times. However, these inspired authors wrote according to the mores and languages of their day. That is why interpretation is necessary for each and every age.

The writings that form the Bible were written at different times by many different authors over a period of 1100 years, for diverse purposes, at different places, such as Mesopotamia, Babylonia, Greece, Egypt, Corinth, Ephesus, Rome, and Palestine. Today's biblical scholars continue to work in trying to convey the original message of the Bible into the language and understanding of today's cultures throughout the world.

The Old Testament is the story of God's agreement with Abraham and how Abraham's people (later known as Israelites) struggled to form a nation of faithful followers who worshipped the one true God. The Old Testament is made up of three main parts: the Law; the Prophets, and the Writings. The Law contains rules for conduct, worship, and the beginnings of Israel as a nation. The Prophets contain the history of the twelve tribes of Israel and God's prophecies. The Writings are full of history, laws, poetry, songs, parables, prophecies, philosophy, and wisdom for living.

While the Old Testament is important, the New Testament is made up of the books used within the Christian faith. It is the story of the birth, life, death, resurrection, and ascension of Jesus Christ and his message to all humankind. It is filled with stories about Jesus's missionary activities, teaching, preaching, healing, as well as the missionary activities of his disciples and followers, and their inspired lives and writings to new Christian converts throughout the world.

The New Testament has four main parts: the Gospels; the Acts of the Apostles; the Epistles; and Revelation. The Gospels of Matthew, Mark, Luke, and John tell the stories of Jesus Christ while he was here on Earth. These books include his teachings and are the very foundation of the New Testament. The Acts of the Apostles is the story of the early

Christian church, how its missionaries, like Peter, Paul, and others, spread Christianity throughout the known world. The Epistles are letters written to the church by various authors; some attributed to Peter, others to Paul, and others unknown. Revelation is John's vision of the great struggle between Christ's church and Satan, and the final victory of the Kingdom of God that will come at some future date.

The Bible has influenced the course of Western Civilization more than any other writing in history. Its political development, its great works of literature, its ideas about truth, justice, and the purpose of life continue to influence the world today and seek to make civilization more humane as the years go by.

For the Jewish people, the Old Testament is the Holy Book. For Christians, it is both the Old and New Testaments. Together they form the basis of our religious belief, the truth revealed by God, the truth about God, a set of principles for living according to God's plan, the basis of worship, and sacred writings about the development of a people called Israel and the New Israel, known today as the church. The Bible as we know it was compiled slowly over a long period of years. The historical process by which the biblical canon (meaning the books accepted by the church with divine authority) was compiled continued for more than two centuries after the last book appeared.

Jewish rabbis compiled the Old Testament canon near the close of the first century A.D. The early Christian church, in the second century A.D., increasingly recognized the inspiration of Old Testament books and came to accept and use them in Christian services in apostolic times. The canons significance was seen in relation to Christ and his mission. They nurtured the prayer life of the people as well as provided a way of seeing life differently.

Early in the third century, church leaders began to make a distinction between the Apocryphal books (those without divine authority) as separate from the books of the Old Testament; however, they continued to use both. Then in the fourth century, local religious ruling bodies decided to include all seventy-two books that made up the Old Testament, the New Testament, and the Apocrypha in what was to become known as the Canon. However, Jerome, a biblical translator, monastic leader, and one of the most influential Latin fathers, disagreed concerning the sacred nature of the apocryphal books because of their content. Nevertheless, traditional acceptance won out. Finally, Reformation Protestants rejected these seven books of the earlier Canon (the Apocrypha), recognizing them as containing elements of truth but not sacred and inspired as were the others. In 1545, at the Council of Trent, the Roman Catholic Church approved a list of canonical books that included the apocryphal books. In 1672, the Eastern Orthodox Church at the Synod of Jerusalem accepted the disputed books, except for Baruch and Maccabees 1 and 2. The Anglican Church accepted all the books of the Apocrypha.

By 100 A. D., the Gospels had been written and they were being widely circulated. In 130 A.D., Marcion, a leading Christian teacher, put in print his heretical ideas with his list of "sacred" books. At the same time, he refused to acknowledge that any Jewish scriptures had anything to do with Christianity. This action made church leaders keenly aware of the need for a church-authorized list of books. Therefore, in 180 A. D., the church fathers published the Muratorian Canon. It was a tentative list of inspired books that included the Gospels, Paul's letters, Acts, Jude, John and Revelation.

By 200 A. D., Christian beliefs were being threatened by Gnosticism, a heretical doctrine that taught that a secret esoteric and mysterious knowledge was necessary for salvation. To deal with this rising heresy, the church called together leaders to consider which books were sacred, those written by the apostles or those close to them, all of which were being used in worship at that time. Early in the third century, Origen, a priest, addressed the concerns and listed books as acknowledged (universally accepted), disputed (finally accepted), and rejected (those declared ordinary). Finally, to put this dispute to rest, Anthanasius, Bishop of Alexandria, resolved all arguments with his list of those books we have in our Bible today. The process of canonization (from the Greek *kanon*, meaning standard, rule or guide indicates that the church selected the sixty-six books we know as the Bible today as the norm of life and thought, as well as the intention of distinguishing God's truth from many of the false and heretical teachings that were taking place. Thus, we can read the Bible with assurance that the words are truly inspired by God.

The first Bibles were only available in Greek and Hebrew. Later translations were needed as Christianity spread to other lands. The Latin Vulgate became the first official translation and Pope Damasus I appointed Jerome, a well-respected church father, to translate the authorized Latin version. He used the original Hebrew Scriptures for the basis of his translation. It was the customary version of the Bible for over 1,000 years, and is still used by the Roman Catholic Church today.

Latin's decline as the dominate language of Europe meant that common laypeople no longer were able to read the Bible. This required translations to be written and these continue today. The Roman Catholic Church disdained and rejected many of the early translations. Some translators were even put to death. Translation into English started as early as 1382 with John Wycliffe, an Oxford seminary professor, scholastic philosopher, theologian, Biblical translator, and reformer. He was an influential dissident within the Roman Catholic priesthood during the fourteenth century. He was condemned as a heretic, and additional unauthorized translations were prohibited under pain of excommunication.

Luther believed that the people deserved the right to read and study Scripture, and therefore translated the Bible into German, to the disapproval of the Roman Catholic Church. William Tyndale, Myles Coverdale, and others took up this same undertaking. King James, in 1611, along with fifty scholars, published a translation now renowned for its beautiful language, though it is difficult to read in this era. Translations of the Bible continue today in an effort to make the Bible more understandable for succeeding generations. Today one can choose among numerous English translations, which in 2017 included 670 languages. However, the Bible is only efficacious if read and studied.

NOTES

CHAPTER 4

How to Read the Bible

More people have read the Bible than any other book since time began. It was written originally in Hebrew and Greek, but today has been translated into more than 6,500 different languages and dialects. When a book is published, if it has sales of million or more copies, publishers think it has done very well. But every year, there are 500 million or more copies of the Bible published and that alone should say this book contains something very important. Indeed it does!

The Bible deals with the great questions that people are forever asking, such as: Where did we come from? Where are we going? What does life mean? What should we be doing while here? What is wrong and what is right? Who is God? How do we come to an understanding of this universe?

Now other great books have dealt with these same questions, but the standard for Christians has always been the Bible because it comes closer to answering them. You see, the Bible deals with these questions in the context of real people and their lives. It tells about people just as they were, what they thought, and what they did. It tells when they saw clearly and walked straight and when they blundered and went wrong. It tells when they followed their own leanings and yearnings with disastrous results and when they caught a glimpse of God that made the way altogether different.

Little by little God is revealed to us by the way God reveals himself and is reflected in the lives of the people of the Bible. Finally, one great person arises in the pages of Holy Scripture who is Jesus the Messiah. He becomes the hero of the whole story. He is the climax of the Bible and final image of God's truth and love. In looking at Jesus, people of all times and in every place of the world have said: "This is what God must be like."

Through the centuries, people everywhere have honored the entire Bible because to them it represents the medium for God's work. But at the same time, they have held in high regard certain parts of the Bible more than others because God is revealed more clearly in some places in Scripture than others. In other words, some books of the Bible have more value than other books. This shouldn't be really surprising because the Bible is not merely a book, but a library containing many books with many different authors written over a time span of many centuries. This library contains religious interpretations of history, stories, poetry, hymns, sermons and letters. However, tying it all together there is a golden thread that one cannot miss. It is this: there is a God, God matters, and God makes a difference in your life and mine.

Being ordinary men and women, our knowledge of God is conditioned by the way in which we live and the circumstances surrounding us. The authors of the Bible wrote down everything they thought and observed that revealed the life and spirit of their people that was based upon a covenant or agreement they had with God. What was taking place was the idea of progressive revelation.

To understand this, consider the example of children and how they grow up in the understanding of their parents as they grow and mature in their relationship. A father or mother is seen quite differently to a son or daughter at age two versus age twenty. To affirm progressive revelation does not discredit the Bible when we say some of the things thought about God or even the world have since been corrected. An example would be maps drawn by early European explorers who discovered the New World. They found the new land they sought, but the early maps they drew of it were not always accurate. The coastlines were far different than what they originally thought and modern maps with more information corrected them. This, however, hardly takes away from the most important thing which was showing the way to the New World. And so it is with the Bible. The pioneers showed us the way to God and have given us a path to follow. It doesn't matter that some of their concepts have been changed because the Bible was doing that all along. The later books of the New Testament correct some of the earlier views contained in the Old Testament.

From ancient animal sacrifices and blood offerings to the voice of Micah the prophet who said: "do justice and to love kindness, and walk humbly with your God" (Micah 6:8b) there is the idea of progressive revelation. From Samuel who had the Lord's blessings to slay all the Amalekites to the voice of Jesus saying, "Love your enemies and pray for those who persecute you" (Matthew 5:44) there is progressive revelation. The Bible shows life in process - a journey -with our understanding of God growing as we continue our journey even today. And it is Jesus who illumines and sheds his light on this journey with God.

So considering the above, how is the Bible to be read? The first thing is to begin with Jesus Christ. With most books, the best place to start is at the beginning. Not so with the Bible. This is the last place you want to begin. All the books of the Bible that were written before Jesus appeared on the scene is preparation. All that was written in the Bible after Jesus came is comment. Therefore, to understand the Bible correctly you must begin with an understanding of Jesus Christ. The better understanding of Jesus and his mission one has, the better one is able to understand the history of God's people and Israel that led up to God's ultimate revelation in the coming of Jesus Christ. The biblical writings after Jesus came help us understand what we need to know about our lives, our associations, our hope and our destiny. To read the Bible correctly, you must begin with Jesus.

The best place to start reading the Bible is with the Gospels. The earliest and most straightforward gospel is Mark. That is a good place to start to read the Bible. When finished with Mark, then go on to Luke and then to Matthew and finally to John. This gives one a foundation and an initial perspective about Jesus. If you are going to come to the Bible, come to it first with the perspective of Jesus Christ.

With that perspective in place, one is able to go anywhere else in Scripture they choose remembering all that comes before Jesus is preparation and all that was written after him is comment. But start with Jesus.

Second, you must read the Bible with purpose and that means proper purpose. If you wanted to read a romance you would not pick up a book on mathematics. If you wanted to read history you would not look to Shakespeare. Said another way, one should not seek to impose their meaning and purpose on the Bible. One must let the Bible impose its message and purpose on you.

Some read the Bible expecting to find great literature, and while the Bible does have some glowing passages in the realm of letters, the biblical authors would have been dismayed at the suggestion that their writings had a literary purpose. The danger in reading the Bible as literature is that it distracts the reader from the Bible's deeper intent to convey to us the words and wisdom of God.

Over the past five decades conflict has arisen which discredits both science and religion brought about by seeing the Bible as book of science. However, the words of Psalm 139 are true whether one thinks the earth is round or flat. The parable of the prodigal son is the story of us all and is not falsified by the theory of evolution. Science, however necessary, is perceived by the senses and cannot completely understand the depths of the human soul. Science is analytical, and cannot serve the wholeness of our nature. It can give answers to how, but none to why. Only faith can ultimately say why. Therefore, the Bible is not a book of science and to use it for such purposes is misguided. It has a much mightier business at hand.

Others read the Bible as if it is a road map to the end and a prediction of the future. They find happy hunting ground in the books of Revelation and Daniel, which. These two books can become the focus of their religion with the rest of the Bible being used to shed light on the mysteries of the end times. One wonders why. Jesus said that kind of seeking is futile, for only the Father knows when the end will come. Why speculate over what cannot be known?

Then there are those who use the Bible to forecast or guide their movements. Like the fellow who would open his Bible every morning, put his finger on a verse, and use that as a guide for the day. He did this one morning and found himself reading "Judas hung himself." Well that didn't sit well with him, so he tried again. That time his finger landed on the verse, "Go and do likewise."

The Bible is also not a history textbook. Certainly, there is history recorded in it, but the authors were not concerned with writing an objective account of historic events. Their concern was to write God's story and pointing out how certain nations and individuals were apprehended by God and the impact that on them and the events of the time.

Third, the Bible is also not meant to be read critically. Modern critical Biblical scholarship is great, but it never comes to an end. Critical biblical scholarship is open to mistakes and is never complete. As the old saying goes, wisdom can tarry as the facts multiply. The meaning behind the words and phrases of the Bible can lead to a study of Hebrew and Greek. The study of the background of biblical events soon involves archaeology, anthropology, and other inquiries of like scope. Serious Bible scholars, who do wonderful work for us all, have all sorts of critical disciplines which they use to study the scriptures, but there is just no way for the average person to bring the scope of all these to their Bible reading. A little background as to when and by whom and why the book was written is helpful, and perhaps even essential. But the Bible should be read with a wide-angle lens, not a microscope. Look at the big picture and seek the essential message, lest you miss the forest for the trees.

If someone paints a picture and shows it to you, you don't stand very close to it for the painting to make its impression on your mind. You stand back from it so that the whole picture becomes part of the mind's image. If someone showed you one piece of a jigsaw puzzle it wouldn't mean much. However, when all the pieces are put together you are able to see the whole picture. So read the whole story. Don't get caught up in the small details.

Also, don't hone in on one verse alone to the exclusion of the surrounding context. Take for example the well-known words of St. Paul, "I can do all things in him (Christ) who strengthens me." (Philippians 4:13). It is not like Christ is Popeye's trusty can of spinach which gives superhuman strength and ability to do things beyond reason. One shouldn't attempt brain surgery just because the Bible says: "I can do all things through Christ who strengthens me." This is the problem with taking individual verses or small bits in the Bible out of context. The context in the above passage is clearly contentment and the power Christ supplies to enable us to face times of plenty and times of want.

Fourth, read the Bible with imagination. Put yourself in the story. Try to be present as if you were actually there at each event watching. This is especially true with the stories involving Jesus or the ones that he told. Read the story as if you were actually present. What is its message? What is Jesus saying? How might it apply to you? Let the story make its impression upon your mind. When you do, you will find that Jesus presents you not so much with propositions and arguments as with pictures. Jesus spoke mostly in pictures that made people think.

Once while in a crowd of people, a lawyer asked Jesus: "who is my neighbor?" Jesus answered not with a legal definition of a neighbor, but rather with a picture. He told a story of a traveler who was beaten and robbed and left for dead in a roadside ditch. People of high standing in the religious community of the day who should have stopped to help, passed him by. A man from the region of Samaria who wasn't expected to help, did. He treated the man's wounds, got him to safety and paid for his care. When Jesus gave this mental picture about who was a true neighbor, the lawyer was able to answer his own question.

And last, read the Bible devotionally. It is here you are opening up your soul — your very being — to the book's healing light. You are not just seeking information, but seeking the person of Jesus, who in the process will end up finding you.

For instance, consider the story of Jesus and Zacchaeus (Luke 19: 1-0). Read it devotionally and ask yourself: How does this apply to me? When you do, you will find you have not been reading about Jesus and Zacchaeus, but about Jesus and you.

Zacchaeus was a tax collector, very short in stature, who was a collaborator with Rome and so hated by his own people. One day in Jericho, Zacchaeus climbed up a tree to better be able to see Jesus passing by. Upon seeing Zacchaeus in that unusual spot, Jesus invites himself to Zacchaeus' home for dinner. Jesus makes no criticism of him, but in the very presence of Christ, Zacchaeus in effect thinks: "I have got to do something about my life." Might this story apply to you? Maybe it's you that is up a tree. Ever been there? Maybe it is you who feel despised, alone, neglected, or rejected. Ever been there? Maybe for the first time in your life, in the presence of Christ, you feel it is possible to do something about your life. Maybe you read the story and hear Jesus saying to you, "I want to come to where you live. I want to be with you." And maybe you'll hear someone who loves you even when you can't love yourself. Someone who believes in you, even when you no longer believe in yourself. It is this picture that enables you to see and understand how Jesus can touch your life. This is the picture that shows you who can heal you and bring you back to a new way of living, a new way of loving and definite ways of serving. It can happen. It has for countless millions down through the ages.

Remember then, when reading the Bible, begin with Christ! Read with proper purpose. Do not read it critically, but imaginatively and devotionally. In so doing you will know God because God will find you.

NOTES

CHAPTER 5

A Short History of Baptism

The Lutheran Church recognizes two sacraments: baptism and the Lord's Supper. According to Martin Luther and his understanding of the scriptures, there are three criteria that make something a sacrament: 1) Christ must command it; 2) It must carry an eternal promise; and 3) it must use an earthly element.

What makes baptism and the Lord's Supper essential factors in the life of the Church is not only their historical basis, but also their chief meanings. The belief the church stands upon is that the sacraments, in the form of action, furnish a complete expression of the central content of the gospel and are naturally connected with the events of Christ. The sacraments appear to Christian faith as the self-impartation of divine love in the form of action. The two principal features that characterize this divine love are connected in baptism and the Lord's Supper.

Baptism reveals the charisma of divine love as unprompted prevenient grace (a grace apart from anything a human has done). It is the sacrament of "prevenient" love. The Lord's Supper reveals the self-giving of divine love in the event of Christ's life, death, and resurrection. It is the sacrament of vicarious suffering and victorious love. Therefore, the sacraments are not only historical institutions, but rather continual actions of divine love, grace, and mercy wholly imparted by God in Christ alone.

Baptism is first and foremost God's action. Baptism unites us with the risen Christ and makes us members of God's family. Through water united with the power of God's creative and redeeming word, the waters of baptism wash away and cleans the guilt of our sins, confer upon us God's grace, deliver us from the power of death, and assure us eternal life in God's Kingdom. Therefore, baptism is a sign of God's love, and God wills that we be reborn in the image of Christ the Savior. Baptism is also an act by which God enables us to live according to the guidance of the Holy Spirit. Baptism brings us closer to God and marks the beginning of our spiritual journey in life. It is an act through which the church receives and integrates new members into its fellowship. Baptism is then primarily an *action* of God, with respect to which the church's act is a *reaction*.

Baptism is a lifelong journey. God walks with us on this journey, forgives us when we fail and fall, and sends us the gifts of the Holy Spirit. Baptism lets us share in the life of Jesus Christ, who died on the cross that we might have new life. Baptism also brings us closer to others. Through baptism we are reborn children of God and inheritors of eternal life. We become brothers and sisters in a new family that includes Christians all over the world. The grace we receive at baptism helps us throughout life to form relationships with others based on love, mutual respect, and forgiveness. As St. Paul said, "[T]herefore if anyone is in Christ, he is a new creation; the old has passed away, behold, the new has come." (2 Cor.5.17)

John, a cousin of Jesus and known as the baptizer, baptized people in the Jordan River. Unlike earlier washings in the Old Testament, John's manner of baptism summoned people to repentance. This was God's way of preparing people for the coming of the Messiah who would forgive their sins. Jesus own baptism by John is recorded in Mark 1:9-11; Matthew 3:13-17; and Luke 3:21-22. When Jesus came out of the water, a voice spoke from heaven and the Holy Spirit, descending in the form of a dove, filled him. People's failure to obey God and love each other is what brought on their subjection to eternal suffering and death. Only Jesus succeeded in loving God and people completely. Through baptism, we begin to fulfill God's plan for us by dying with Christ and being raised with Christ. Christ's victory over death is our victory over death. As the scripture says:

> Do you know that all of us who have been baptized into
> Christ Jesus were baptized into his death? We were buried
> therefore with him by baptism into death, so that as Christ
> was raised from the dead by the glory of the Father, we too
> might walk in newness of life. For if we have been united
> with him in a death like his, we shall certainly be united
> with him in a resurrection like his. We know that our old
> self was crucified with him so that the sinful body might
> be destroyed, and we might no longer be enslaved to sin.
> (Rom. 6:3-6)

Through baptism we receive God's promise of salvation. At the same time, we receive the faith we need to be open to God's grace in our lives. In this way, baptism prepares us for eternal life. "For by grace you have been saved through faith, and this is not your own doing; it is a gift from God." (Eph. 2:8)

Baptism is the door to life in Jesus Christ. When we receive the gift of the Holy Spirit in baptism, we enter a new life based on the power and authority of God's love. "Truly, truly, I say to you, he who hears my word and believes him who sent me, has eternal life; he does not come into judgment, but has passed from death to life." (John 5:24)

Water is the physical element used in baptism, which cleanses and renews us. Through water, God promises the person receiving baptism eternal life. And how can water do such great things?

As Martin Luther says to us in the Small Catechism:

> Clearly the water does not do it but the Word of God,
> which is with, in, and among the water, and faith, which
> trusts this Word of God in the water For without the
> Word of God the water is plain water and not a baptism,
> but with the Word of God it is a baptism, that is, a grace-
> filled water of life and a "bath of the new birth in the Holy
> Spirit." St. Paul says: "He saved us, not because of any
> works of righteousness that we had done, but according to

his mercy, through the water of rebirth and renewal by the Holy Spirit. This Spirit he poured out on us richly through Jesus Christ our Savior, so that, having been justified by his grace, we might become heirs according to the hope of eternal life. The saying is sure." (Titus 3:5-8) **7.** God's word at once then, is the source of life and the power that gives life. This can be seen from the very beginning of the Bible, for God created the world by his word.[5]

Through the gospel and the sacraments, Christ is present in the church. In baptism, God's word is present in the name of the Father and of the Son and of the Holy Spirit. Infants and children are baptized in the Lutheran Church and other protestant denominations so that they might receive the benefits of God's grace, freedom from sin, and the guidance of the Holy Spirit. Even though they can't verbally accept God, Lutherans believe that God gives the gift of love to all who receive the sacrament, including infants and children. Lutherans, as we read earlier, call this prevenient grace, meaning God calls our name and bestows his approval for us, even before we are able to call upon his name. "But when Jesus saw it he was indignant, and said to them, Let the little children come to me, do not hinder them; for to such belongs the kingdom of God. Truly, I say to you, whoever does not receive the kingdom of God like a child shall not enter it." Mark 10:14-15).

The scriptures tell us that Paul baptized whole households, and based upon this we believe that infants were part of many households. While this is an argument from silence, it is a very good argument. Once you receive the sacrament of holy baptism, it is forever. The Lutheran church will honor any other Christian denomination's baptism.

Lutherans baptize by pouring or sprinkling, although immersion is the best symbolism when it comes to rising and dying with Christ. Christian author and preacher Fredrick Buechner gives us a delightful understanding of baptism: "Baptism consist of getting dunked or sprinkled. Which technique is used matters about as much as whether you pray kneeling or standing on your head. Dunking is a better symbol, however. Going under symbolizes the end of everything about your life that is less than human. Coming up again symbolizes the beginning in you of something strange and new and hopeful. You can breathe again."[6]

Buechner then addresses baptism, by asking two questions:

"How about infant baptism? Shouldn't you wait until the child grows up enough to know what's going on? Answer: "If you don't think there is as much of the less-than-human in an infant as there is in anybody else, you have lost touch with reality. When it comes to the forgiving and transforming love of God, one wonders if the six-week old screecher knows all that much less than the Archbishop of Canterbury about what's going on."[7]

Lutherans, therefore, believe that God can work through three drops of water just as well as through a tub full. It is God's word with water that is important, not the amount of water used. So, baptism is a key to the Christian's life whereby we enter the church of Christ, and is, therefore, necessary for one to be a Christian. "And now why do you wait. Rise up and be baptized, and wash away our sins, calling on his name." (Acts: 22:16)

NOTES

CHAPTER 6

What it Means to Be Baptized

Holy baptism is rooted in the command of Jesus Christ and the tradition of the early church. It is on this premise alone that the church baptizes. Jesus' cousin John baptized him at the very beginning of his ministry in the river Jordon. We know this as a fact because of the synoptic gospels, Matthew, Mark and Luke, which all record this event. Yet, at the same time, we are also aware of the difficulty Jesus' baptism caused the writers.

It was felt early on that to be baptized by someone like John made you a follower of that person, i.e., a disciple. So, Jesus' baptism presented a dual problem of a sinless Jesus, submitting to John's baptism for the remission of sins, and John baptizing Jesus being interpreted as making Jesus John's follower. However, note what happens in the Gospels. Mark, who wrote first, records the incident of Jesus' baptism. He writes in a very straightforward manner. He says "In those days Jesus came from Nazareth of Galilee and was baptized by John in the Jordan." (Mark1:9) That's it.

Turning our attention to Matthew, we hear him say, "Then Jesus came from Galilee to the Jordan to John, to be baptized by him. John would have prevented him, saying, "I need to be baptized by you, and do you come to me?" (Matthew 3:13-14) Matthew seems to recognize the problem and tries to offer a bit of explanation.

The Gospel of Luke seems to take a whole different approach. This depiction of John's baptizing is filled with much detail, and by the time you get to Jesus' baptism, one wonders whether John or someone else baptized Jesus. Luke, to some extent, leaves some doubt in our minds that John was even present at Jesus' baptism. This concern is raised in chapter seven of Luke when John sends his disciples to question and verify Jesus' mission and message. In the Gospel of John, Jesus' baptism is never mentioned. There is absolutely no mention of Jesus being baptized or anyone else for that matter.

So, when you put these facts together, we know for certain that Jesus was baptized by John in the Jordan River. If he had not been, the Gospel writers would not have worked hard to downplay the fact. What do you mean the Son of God was baptized by a mere man, and of all things, for the forgiveness of sins?

We also know from the book of Acts that baptism was practiced in the early church. It was some of the first instructions given to the disciples by Jesus before his ascension and to the Christian converts on the day of Pentecost. Also in the book of Acts is the story of Philip baptizing the Ethiopian eunuch, who was moved by Philip's words. Peter baptized Cornelius, a Roman centurion, and his entire family. Paul baptized whole households of faith. So, then it is a simple fact of Biblical history from the earliest times that Christians have regarded baptism, along with Holy Communion, as ordained by Christ, necessary for salvation, and necessary to the church's mission.

It is important to note that there are two kinds of baptism portrayed in the New Testament. The first is the baptism of John. This was a missionary type of baptism that had about it the idea of a conversion and repentance. It was a preparation for the approaching Kingdom of God, the idea being that if you repent now and change your ways, then when the Kingdom of God comes - which was expected any day - you would be forgiven and granted a place there with God. However, the Kingdom did not come as soon as John and others expected it would. In fact, it did not come the way they thought it would. So, the idea of baptism underwent a shift in thought from preparation for the last day to incorporation into the Christian faith. It became an entry rite into the Christian family whose members would sustain and nurture one another in the example of Christ. These two concepts of baptism are practiced today.

In some traditions, baptism is delayed until an older age when the child is cognizant of his or her sin and recognizes their need for forgiveness. It has about it the idea of repentance, change, and decision. When that is recognized, one accepts responsibility for one's own faith in a public ceremony, which usually is baptism by immersion. That is basically the tradition that comes from John's baptism. The largest body within the Christian tradition, the Baptist Church, gets its name from John the Baptist.

The other baptismal tradition comes out of the teaching of Paul. This tradition is taught and recognized by the Lutheran church, along with Methodists, Presbyterians, Episcopalians, Roman Catholics and many other denominations. We hold to the baptism of incorporation into the body of Christ and into the family of believers. The idea of the forgiveness of sins is still within this tradition, as is a promise that can and must be relied upon: the promise of eternal life. Also, within the Pauline tradition is the fact that all people — infants, children, and adults — are received into church membership by baptism.

The congregation that one is baptized into is responsible for nurturing and training with respect to all that the Christian life has to offer. In other words, there are certain privileges and responsibilities that go along with belonging to the church, and these things need to be learned and lived out. These are the reasons Lutherans baptize infants. Lutherans want young children to be a part of the family of God, brought up in Christian love and care and concern and having the privilege of joy of life with God from the very beginning. This is why it makes little sense for parents to bring their child for baptism and then never bring the child back to church to learn what it all means. Mind you, the baptism is still valid, the gift is still given, but it loses its potency because the gift is never explored. It's like giving an Alka Seltzer tablet to someone with no water. You have to put the tablet in the water to get some fizz out of the thing! In the same way, you have to bring the child to church to get some real nourishment and life out of baptism. Baptism is then an outward sign, a visible word, and a demonstration of an inward grace. Simply put, it is God showing us that God loves us. What it is not is a hell prevention vaccination!

Water is the earthly element used in the sacrament of baptism. (Luther defined a sacrament as an ordinance of the church which was established by Jesus, which used an element of the earth and which conveyed an eternal promise) Some people are curious about how much water is necessary. The answer is that no amount of water is specified in the Bible. There is also no account in the scriptures that indicates how baptism should be administered. Because John the Baptist preached at the River Jordan, some have concluded that his converts were immersed in the waters of the river. Yet early pictures and paintings of the baptism of Christ show him standing in the water while John poured water over his head.

Most Christians believe that sprinkling or pouring is quite sufficient for baptism, though immersion is proper for those who desire it. An important point to understand is that it would be erroneous to make the sacrament of holy baptism dependent on how much water is used, how it is administered, or what temperature the water might should be. Lutherans believe that God can work through any amount of water that he chooses, and that the amount does not hinder the working of the Holy Spirit. Water is only the symbol - a sign that has no power in and of itself. The power of baptism comes when God's word is joined with water and the promises are made.

Now we can be sure that early Christians were baptized in streams and pools. But in the cities, when many wanted to be baptized at one time, they most likely were baptized at fountains using vessels of water. People spoke of baptism as the divine fountain through which comes the water of salvation, so these vessels became known as fountains or fonts, many of which were carved out of stone. Others were made out of lead, copper, or bronze. Some were quite large and enabled the person being baptized to go down into the water.

In later centuries, when great cathedrals were built, the fonts were covered and called baptisteries. They were located in what was known as the mother church. In early Catholic cathedrals, the bishop functioned there, so that is where the baptistery was located – at the mother church - and where the people were baptized. Later, it became a rule that a font should be located in each house of worship.

In earlier days, the fonts were located adjoining the nave of the church. However, now, the emphasis is on locating the font near the entry way to the church to remind those who enter that holy baptism is the sacrament of entrance to the Christian life. As we are made citizens of the nation first and foremost by birth, so by the birth given in holy baptism we are made citizens of the Kingdom of God. As we enter the church and see the font, we are reminded that we are baptized Christians and that we are part of God's people.

Other questions come to mind out of certain practices within baptism. Is baptism once and for all? The answer is yes. The concept of rebaptism (being baptized a second or third time) is foreign in the Christian faith. Just as you were literally born once, you are spiritually born once and for all by baptism. The idea of a second baptism actually becomes a problem because it calls into question the validity of the first baptism. Were the promises of God in one's first baptism invalidated in some way? Do we need two baptisms for us to trust God's promises? What then about three or even four? Yes, some churches do re-baptize, but that really seems to show they must feel the validity of baptism is found not in the promises of God, but in the amount of water to be used or an age of accountability. When this occurs, it is based on a human action rather than a God action. Frankly, it makes no sense.

The rite of baptism is full of symbolism, too. Look at all the different sizes and shapes of fonts used. When the font is raised up on one step it reminds us that there is one God, one Lord, one baptism for the remission of sins A font raised up on three steps is symbolic of the Holy Trinity (Father, Son and Holy Spirit) in whose three-fold name we baptize. When the font is in the shape of a circle, it becomes the symbol of eternity and reminds us that eternal life begins with baptism. A font with four sides is symbolic of the fact that children of God enter the Kingdom from the north, south, east and west, and that Jesus commanded his disciples to baptize all nations. An octagonal (eight -sided) font symbolizes that baptism has taken the place of the Jewish rite of circumcision where on the eighth day after the birth of a male Jew, he was received into the faith and dedicated to the Lord. Eight was also the number of regeneration, so an eight-sided font is symbolic of a new creation and a new birth, both of which baptism represents.

In the early church, the font was richly carved and decorated with beautiful and costly symbols. This was done to remind the people of the priceless value of every child of God. When we see the baptismal font in the church, we should be reminded that we too have been baptized and that the promises given are true and sure, and that we can rely on them. We should also be reminded that we are cleansed from sin through forgiveness, and that we are members of the one body of Christ, the church. As baptized children of God, we are inheritors of eternal life. As such, we remember too that our baptismal association carries with it a responsibility, a sacred trust, to live together in Christian love and in keeping with God's holy will.

What then is the importance of baptism? In baptism, the mother and father into whose keeping God has dared commit a little soul come to dedicate the child to God. They come to tell God that though they have great dreams for this little one and are prepared to pinch for years so that this child might have a chance out of all the possibilities that life offers. What they are asking and praying for is that for all their days they might first belong to Jesus Christ. And if they are sincere, then it makes a tremendous difference in the child's life – for the way the twig is bent, the branch is apt to grow. In baptism, therefore, one should keep their eyes not on the child or the parents of the child, but on God. In baptism, God takes the child in his arms and says, "I live and I gave myself for you. I have plans for you. I have been waiting for you. My love will surround you and spend itself on you. I will guard you, guide you, and comfort you. I will bring you safely through. You will never be on your own. I will never leave you to your own resources because now you are mine and I will be with you always." Hopefully that knowledge and belief in a person's life can make all the difference in the world as to how they approach and experience life.

The sacrament of holy baptism given to each of us individually is like a picture of the promise that lies behind it. For Jesus said, "Lo I am with you always, even to the end of the world." (Matthew 28:20) It has potency not only at the time of the ceremony, but throughout life. God's words have hands and feet and will always reach for his children and run after them. So, baptism chases us down through the years, and every time we are witness to a baptism, it reminds us that we were baptized, as well. In baptism, we have become part of a wonderful love story in which God goes on loving us with a patience that never gives out and never gives up. Its set purpose is to deliver us from our old sinful selves and make us new people in Christ.

NOTES

CHAPTER 7

A Short History of Holy Communion

Holy Communion is the second of two sacraments within the Lutheran Church. In Holy Communion one receives the body and blood of Jesus Christ through bread and wine. Jesus instituted this sacrament. It is a reminder of the last meal shared by Jesus and his disciples during the Jewish Passover before Jesus went to the cross to die. It is a visual reminder and remembrance of Jesus' death on the cross and brings us to the realization that eternal life will be ours. It is experiencing God's grace by which the gifts of forgiveness, life, and salvation come to us.

The sacrament of the Lord's Supper supports our participation in the life and work of the church. It is a gift from God with no strings attached, given not only for our personal benefit, but also for the benefit of all who receive it in faith. This sacrament is a source of strength that empowers us to better serve God, others, and His church. Holy Communion renews our faith and trust in God who remains constant and faithful in a rapidly changing and uncertain world.

The roots of our faith are found in the sacrament of Holy Communion. Like baptism, Holy Communion is a real and physical means of understanding this gift of God to us. As we partake of this sacrament, we are able to live with the assurance that God's love, grace, and mercy are given to us. It is a confidence-building sacrament. Receiving Holy Communion also gives us spiritual nourishment, which every Christian needs. And what is the benefit of such eating and drinking? Luther says in the Small Catechism, "The words 'give for you' and 'shed for you….for the forgiveness of sin' show us that forgieveness of sin, life, and salvation are given to us in the sacrament through these words because where there is forgivness of sins, there is also life and salvation"[8] So, as baptism makes us children of God, receiving Holy Communion is the sustaining sacrament that nourishes and strengthens the relationship we have with God that began in baptism.

The Old Testament is where Holy Communion has its origin. The Old Testament tells the story about the first Passover meal shared by Moses and the Israelites right before he led the people out of Egypt and, in turn, out of slavery. God instructed the Israelites, through Moses, to mark their door frames with the blood of a slaughtered lamb. The angel of death (which was the tenth plague or judgement visited on Egypt because of Pharaoh's refusal to let the people of Israel go) would then pass over those homes while claiming the lives of all first-born Egyptian children. When the people of Israel gathered that night to eat their last meal, they shared roasted lamb (symbolizing sacrifice), unleavened bread (representing their hasty flight out of Egypt), and bitter herbs (recalling the suffering of slavery). God commanded that the Passover be celebrated each year on the anniversary of the Exodus from Egypt. The Jews celebrate it to this day. "[T]his day shall come for you memorial day, and you shall keep it as a feast to the Lord; throughout your generations you shall observe it as an ordiance forever."(Exod. 12:14)

The New Testament pronounces another Passover meal. Jesus, on the night before his crucifixion, gathered with his twelve disciples to celebrate the Jewish Passover. During that final meal, Jesus instituted the sacrament of the Lord's Supper. Jesus blessed and broke bread, saying, "Take, eat, this is my body." (Matt. 26:27-28) Jesus also gave them a cup of wine, saying, "Drink of it, all of you; for this is my blood of the covenant which is poured out for manyfor the forgiveness of sins." (Matt. 26:27-28) On that night, Jesus changed the meaning of the Passover meal forever.

The comparisons between the Exdous story and the Last Supper is important for Christians to understand. There would be no Last Supper as we know it were it not for the Exdous story. In the Exodus story, deliverance for Israel was from the bondage of slavery. At the Last Supper, deliverance was changed to deliverance from sin for the Christian. Israel, in the Exodus story, was given new life in the wilderness. At the Last Supper, Christians are given new life in Christ. In the Exodus story the blood of the lamb saved people from death. In the Last Supper, Christ dying as the lamb of God saves us from death. In the Exodus story what God had done for Israel was to be remembered. In the Last Supper what Christ did on the cross for us is to be remembered. According to the the Exodus story, Israel was made a new nation. According to the Last Supper, we are made a new community of God's people. Jesus chose to become the Passover or Paschal lamb. Therefore Jesus' blood marked the wooden cross on which he was crucified, like the doorposts were marked when God's people fled Egypt. Once more the angel of death passed over us because of Christ's death on the cross. This time eternal life was made possible, as Jesus promised earlier. Scripture says, "I am the living bread that came down from heaven, whoever eats of this bread will live forever; and the bread that I will give for the life of the world is my flesh." (John 6:51)

Communion is a celebration of joy. On this joyful occasion, the continuing presence of Christ in our lives and God's concern for people on earth give us much to celebrate. Communion is an act of sharing and caring. Through this sacrament, we can share with others the gifts Jesus so willingly gives us. It is known as the *Eucharist,* a Greek word meaning thanksgiving.

Again Fedrick Beuchner puts a wonderful twist on the Lord's Supper. In *Wishful Thinking: A Seekers ABC,* he shares these words:

> It is make believe. You make believe that the one who breaks the bread and blesses the wine is not the plump parson who smells of William's Aqua Velva but Jesus of Nazareth. You make believe that the tasteless wafer and the cheap port are his flesh and blood. You make believe that by swallowing them your are swallowing his life into

your lifeand that there is nothing in earth or heaven more important for you to do than this. It is a game you play because he said to play it. "Do this in remembrance of me." Do this. Play that it makes a difference. Play that it makes sense. If it seems a childish thing to do, do it in remembrance that you are a child.....To eat this particular meal together is to meet at the level of our most basic humanness, which involves our need not just for food but for each other. I need you to fill my emptiness just as you need me to help fill yours. As for the emptiness that's still left over, well, we're in it together, or it in us. Maybe it's most of what makes us human and makes us brothers and sisters.[9]

When we receive the Lord's Supper we receive Christ's body and blood. When we receive the Lord's Supper we praise God in our words and our songs. While baptism is the beginning of our life in Christ, the Lord's Supper supports and maintains our relationship with God and continues to strengthen us throughout life. The confession of sins should always precede receiving the sacrament of the Lord's Supper. Confession of sins is done publically within the worship service (or home communions). where the congregation acknowledges its sinfulness together. It is not just individual sins that are confessed, but the sins of the whole people of God. The pastor grants absolution or forgiveness after the prayer of confession has been offered. Confession can also be a private matter, which is a more personal way of receiving God's grace. Luther rightly taught that Christ is truly present in the sacrament of Holy Communion.

Because bread and wine were offered by Jesus when he instituted the Lord's Supper, it is still offered today by Lutheran congregations and other denominations. Both these elements are the products of God's good earth: bread coming from wheat and wine from grapes. The bread represents the needs of life and the wine represents the amenities of life.

Though the bread remains bread and the wine remains wine, Christ becomes present "in, with, and under" these earthly elements, according to Luther. Scriptures is clear on this:

> As they were eating, he took bread, and blessed, and broke it, and gave it to them, and said, 'Take; this is my body.' And he took a cup and when he had given thanks he gave it to them, and they all drank of it. And he said to them, 'This is my blood of the covenant, which is poured out for many. Truly I say to you, I shall not drink again of the fruit of the vine until that day when I dering it new in the kingdom of God.'" (Mark: 14:22-25)

This great mystery cannot be fully explained. Although we can never fully understand it, we take Christ at his word, believing and affirming that Christ is truly present in the bread and wine.

NOTES

CHAPTER 8

What it Means to Receive
Holy Communion

The sacrament of the Lord's Supper is known by several different names. Among them are Holy Communion, The Eucharist, and the Sacrament of the Altar. One of two sacraments within the Lutheran Church, it too is a means and channel by which God's grace comes to us. The hallmark of Lutheranism is justification by grace through faith.

The Lutheran Church is certainly grace-oriented, but if asked, many people would not be quite sure what this grace is we talk about. Grace is God's unmerited love, given to all people. This love is undeserved, unearned, and free. Grace is the word we use for the concept that God loves us, accepts us, cares for us, forgives us, and gives us the promise of eternal life. Grace is a birthright or inheritance because we are God's children, because we belong to God as sons and daughters. God gives us his grace in the same way an infant is loved dearly by the father and mother, not because the child has done anything to deserve their love, but simply because the child belongs to them.

This grace, this undeserved and unmerited love of God, is not a quantity of God to be given, nor is it a magic potion contained in the bread and wine. Rather it is a quality of God that is shown, given, and received. You can't give a measured quantity of love, but only show or demonstrate by what you do with the quality of feeling that you have. Jesus said, "Greater love has not man than this, that he lay down his life for his friends." (John 15:13)

Grace is something shown us by what God does for us. Beuchner in his marvelous way says in *Wishful Thinking, A Seeker's ABC*:

> After centuries of handling and mishandling, most religious words have become so shopworn nobody's much interested in them anymore. Not so with grace, for some reason. Mysteriously, even derivatives like grace and graceful still have some of the bloom left in them. Grace is something you can never get but only be given. There's no way to earn it or (be deserving of it) or bring it about any more than you can deserve the taste of blackberries and cream or earn good looks or bring about your own birth. A good sleep is grace and so are good dreams. Most tears are grace. The smell of rain is grace. Somebody loving you is grace. Loving somebody is grace. Have you ever tried to love somebody? A crucial eccentricity of the Christian faith is the assertion that people are saved by grace. There's nothing you have to do. There's nothing you have to do. There's nothing you have to do. The grace of God means something like: Here is your life. You might never have been, but you are because the party wouldn't have been complete without you. Here is the world. Beautiful and terrible things will happen. Don't be afraid. I am with you. Nothing can ever separate us. It's for you I created the universe. I love you. There's only one catch. Like any other gift, the gift of grace can be yours only if you'll reach out and take it. Maybe being able to reach out and take it is a gift too.[10]

The sacrament of Holy Communion assures us of forgiveness and acceptance which is very important for our understanding of God. This is reaffirmed time and again when we come to the Lord's Table. Take for example a marriage relationship. A marriage begins with the wedding vows and promises of love. But this love needs to be constantly reaffirmed or the relationship will die, which sadly occurs in today's society. In Holy Communion, God affirms again and again the constancy of His love for us. However, this love shown finds its mark only in the heart that accepts it. In other words, you can never really know what it means to be loved until you are willing to believe that you are. This is most important because this is what makes us worthy or prepared to receive Holy Communion.

Who then receives the sacrament worthily? Luther said, "Fasting and bodily preparation are in fact a fine external discipline, but a person who has faith in these words, 'given for you' and 'shed for you… for the forgiveness of sin,' is really worthy and well prepared. However, a person who does not believe these words or doubts them is unworthy and unprepared, because the words 'for you' require truly believing hearts."[11] So, the one thing you should bring to the table of the Lord is a believing heart, for how can God forgive you your sins if you will not trust him to do so?

Like baptism, there are symbols that are associated with the Lord's Supper. The stalk of wheat reminds us that even as bread is the primary food for physical life, Christ is that food for our souls and spiritual life. One of the most noted passages of Scripture in which we find this idea is:

> Our fathers ate the manna in the wilderness; as it is written, "He gave them bread from heaven to eat." Jesus then said to them, "Truly, truly, I say to you, it was not Moses who have you the bread from heaven; my Father gives you the true bread from heaven. For the bread of God is that which comes down from heaven, and gives life to the world." They said to him, "Lord, give us this bread always." Jesus said to them, "I am the bread of life; he who comes to me shall not hunger, and he who believes in me shall never thirst. (John 6:31-15)

And just as we can receive ordinary bread that has been enriched with vitamins without really understanding the process, so we receive the bread of life without fully comprehending how it has become enriched with the body of our Lord Jesus Christ, although still bread. Indeed, much harm has come to the Christian church because of arguments over just how the bread and wine become or contain the body and the blood, when in fact, we don't really know. We take Christ at his word, "This is my body."

The chalice or the cup is probably the most familiar symbol of this sacrament. While it served as a vessel for wine, notice in the words of institution that it is the cup that is referred to, not the wine. "This is the new Covenant." Jesus referred to this cup as "the cup of blessing" and that was is the third cup that is drunk during the Passover meal. The cup was symbolic of the kind of life that God would pour down upon His children and the experience that would be shared by those in the family of faith. The cup has behind it the idea of shared experience, a future, a destiny, and a hope. In the Garden of Gethsemane, Jesus said, "If it be possible, let this cup pass from me" (Matt. 26.39). The meaning behind His request was let this destiny pass from me.

When James and John wanted to sit at Jesus's side as he came into His Kingdom, he said, "Are you able to drink the cup that I am about to drink?" (Matt. 20:22) In other words, are you able to share in what I have to do, the destiny that is before me? And Jesus replied, "You will drink my cup, but to sit at my right hand and at my left is not mine to grant, but it is for those for whom it has been prepared by my Father." (Matt. 20:23) So, the cup is the shared experience, the unity, the shared destiny that Christians have in Jesus Christ. The chalice or the cup is the new covenant, the new agreement, and the new compact that has been sealed by the blood of Christ for all people. However, now the new covenant would not be an external alliance written on stone as the Ten Commandments were, but rather an internal blood relationship written on the heart of the person whom receives it. In offering the cup, Jesus said, "A new commandment I give to you, that you love one another; even as I have love you, that you also love one another." (John 13:14).

What about the blood? As a kid, did you and a friend ever prick your fingers, rub them together mixing the blood, making you blood brothers or sisters? The notion is that two people receiving a few drops of blood from each other would receive the other's nature and enter into a close personal relationship. When Christians receive the body and blood of Christ, it is a sign of family, a true blood relationship with Jesus Christ. We partake of his nature, so that our sinful nature might constantly be overcome by His more perfect way.

The lamb is also a symbol within the concept of Holy Communion derived from the fact that Christ died during the Passover season when so many lambs were sacrificed at the temple as sin offerings. It was natural for the disciples to think of Christ as the Passover lamb, having sacrificed his life for the sins of the world. The lamb is symbolic of Christ of whom the angel said to Mary, "The Holy Spirit will come upon you, and the power of the Most High will overshadow you; therefore the child to be born will be called holy, the Son of God." (Luke: 1:34) The grapes and wine remind us Jesus said, "I am the vine, you are the branches." (John 15:5a) If we are united with him, we are therefore able to bring forth large amounts of fruit.

Finally, our look at the symbols brings us to the pelican, an unfamiliar symbol for many, yet a very powerful and profound one. This bird will actually prick its breast to feed its young with her blood, which reminds us that Christ willingly shed His blood that He might give life to His children.

Regarding the service of Holy Communion itself, it should be understood that there are a variety of ways the Lord's Supper can be administered. All are equally valid and in no way affect the meaning and the nature of the sacrament. There is nothing holy about the way communion is administered if done reverently. The Bible gives no specifics on how often communion is to be celebrated. Jesus said, "For as often as you eat this bread and drink the cup, you proclaim the Lord's death until he comes." (1 Cor. 11:26) When Holy Communion is included within the worship service, it is a wonderful part of a complete service.

In this fast paced and crazy world that we live in, it important that communion should not be rushed. We should want to take the opportunity to sit amid the silence, the mystery and the majesty of God's grace and the splendor of the church to consider His love, His blessings, and His goodness. We should want to take the time to appreciate the beauty of the earth, the love of family, the joy of friends, the direction of our lives, our plans for tomorrow, and how we can help further His kingdom. What a privilege that is, to know that the Lord of life calls us by name to His table, that we are welcomed, and even more than that, it is our right to be there. Christians can go to the Lords table as a joyful response to his invitation. We should kneel at the Lords table or altar rail when we are able or given the opportunity because this is a Biblical act of worship and a sign of subservience to God. In kneeling, we acknowledge that Christ is master of our lives and the altar is the most common place that one kneels before God when receiving communion.

The linen on the altar is symbolic of the Jesus's shroud or burial cloth and known as the Fair Linen. The linen is what makes the altar an altar, for without it, the altar is no more than a block of ornate wood or stone. Upon the linen are embroidered five marks (usually crosses) which are symbolic of the five wounds of Christ, reminding us of God's greatest intervention on behalf of the human family. Jesus' sacrifice should inspire us to sacrificial living.

The altar is in reality a table, and just like the table in our homes, it is where the family of Christ gathers. It reminds us that in church we are accepted, cared about, and included in the family of God. In Holy Communion, we gather as a family at the table knowing that when we submit to a higher authority, more noble purpose, those things that divide us should fade away and the fellowship of the Holy Spirit is upon us. This most Holy Sacrament reminds us that through it we are not reaching for God, but that through it God is reaching for us. Having been nourished and refreshed by this spiritual food, we leave and go back out into the world that we live in, hearing just before we do, the great promise: "The body and blood of our Lord Jesus Christ strengthen you and keep you in his grace." Always take time to enjoy this most meaningful and blessed service; it is a special and important occasion. Don't complain. It could be thought of like the Burger King commercial, *"Fast Food for Fast Times"* but for the dedicated Christian, it just conflicts too much with the beauty and the majesty that is Holy Communion.

NOTES

_____
_____
_____
_____
_____
_____
_____
_____
_____
_____
_____
_____
_____
_____
_____
_____
_____
_____
_____
_____
_____
_____
_____
_____
_____
_____

CHAPTER 9

A Short History of Lutheran Worship

In Christian worship, God meets his people in a very loving and personal way. This meeting is a two-way communication. In worship, God reveals himself as the creator and loving Father and calls us to gather into the body of Christ for fellowship, support, love, grace, mercy, and forgiveness. Our response to this divine and human encounter takes on such forms as confession, which prepares us for worship, praise, adoration, and thanksgiving. We go to worship to hear God's word for our lives and leave to take that word back out into the world as the hands and feet of Christ that we are called to be. In other words, to be our Lord's present-day disciples. As Luther put it, to be a "little Christ" in the world.

Lutheran worship is not as complicated as many people think. We have freedom, contrary to what some people think, with respect to the rites and ceremonies of the church. It is not necessary that all worship be conducted in the same way, so several different options of services are offered. In the newest Lutheran service book, the Evangelical Lutheran Worship (ELW), there are ten different settings for the Service of Holy Communion. Other services, such as the Service of the Word, the Marriage Service, and the Funeral Service are offered as well. There are also Lenten services (Ash Wednesday and the Sunday of the Passion) and services for the three days (Maundy Thursday, Good Friday, and the Easter Vigil). There are also services of Morning Prayer, Evening Prayer, Night Prayer, and Responsive

Prayer. Additionally, along with the ELW, pastors use what is known as the Occasional Services Book, an edition that contains numerous other services. These additional services or rites, whether simple or elaborate, are great helps to worship.

God uses the common things, such as water, bread, wind, light, symbols, dramatic action, music, paintings, sculpture and architecture as means of His communication to His people and for the enhancement of worship. The important thing is, these rites and symbols should bring people to the gospel and closer to God. They should be performed meaningfully and are not to be seen, as some would hope, to have magical power in them. The power is always in the Word of God, which accomplishes and gives them their specific Christian meaning. Examples are the sacrament of Baptism and the Lord's Supper. We believe that Christ is truly present when we gather for these means of grace. He promises us this in Scripture.

Worship is not the pastor performing before the gathered people, but is the service of the people. Lutherans use a liturgical style of worship. The word liturgy means *work of the people,* but too often in the past the liturgy gave the sense that it was the work of the pastor. The liturgy has always been the responsibility of the people calling people to participation. The liturgy connects the worshiper with the Holy, moving one to action through confession of sins, song, prayer, active listening, sharing of the peace, liturgy assistants, acolytes, crucifers, and banner bearers. Music enhances Lutheran worship and Lutheran composers have contributed greatly to Christian music. The songs and hymns are by no means always on the Christian hit parade, but it really does not take long to learn them. Music must be God-centered and carefully and discriminately chosen. It should exemplify high standards of quality and the texts should reflect the praise of God and the steadfast love of Christ for his church. The message of the text is very important, and the words should help us focus our attention and thoughts on a gracious and loving God.

Attention to the Word (the gospel of Christ) is most important for Lutherans. That is why Lutherans demand good preaching. The sermon should address the needs of sinners and announce the loving activity of

God in people's lives. Sometimes this is the only good news that some people hear in any given week. God is present when humans speak the divine word, so Lutherans gather to hear it together on a regular basis.

Bible reading, Bible study, and prayer, both personal and corporate, are essential to our worship life. Lutherans do not prescribe special postures or mannerisms to accomplish these. Lutherans also see significant life events as occasions for meaningful worship. The church has wisely provided worship forms for these life events as outlined in the Occasional Services book pastors use. These services stress the reality of God in the lives of His people by incorporating personal and family events into the worship life of the congregation. Some of these occasional services are baptism, confirmation, marriage, Commendation of the Dying, burial of the dead, Sending of Holy Communion (to the homebound), Holy Communion in Special Circumstances, Service of Healing, and many others.

Finally, the Lutheran Church follows what is known as the church year for its worship practices. The church year is a calendar of special days and seasons that Christians have followed for centuries. It offers an annual guide for proclaiming and teaching the central truths of Christianity. It is a guide based on the life of Christ.

Each Sunday bears a title related to the church year. Below are the major days or seasons of the church year:

ADVENT: The four Sundays of preparation prior to Christmas are for looking forward to both the birth of Christ and the second coming of Christ.

CHRISTMAS: Falls on December 25 and continues until January 5 in celebration of the birth of Jesus.

EPIPHANY SEASON: Telling of the good news of Christ to the world on four to nine Sundays depending upon the date on which Easter falls each year. Epiphany means a revealing, and what is being revealed during the Epiphany season is who Jesus is: the Son of God.

The LENTEN SEASON: A time of repentance and preparation for Easter lasting forty days, not including Sundays. Ash Wednesday marks the beginning of Lent. Congregates receive the imposition of ashes during the Ash Wednesday service, which reminds us of our frailty and that our bodies, upon death, will return to dust and ashes. There are six Sundays in Lent. The sixth Sunday is known as Palm Sunday or the Sunday of the Passion of Our Lord. This marks the beginning of Holy Week, which consists of Maundy Thursday and Good Friday. Some congregations end Holy Week with the Vigil of Easter held on Saturday night.

EASTER DAY: This is a moveable day and is always the first Sunday after the first full moon of the vernal equinox, which occurs on either March 19, 20, or 21 every year. Easter is the most high and holy day of the church year and celebrates Christ's resurrection. Christmas would have no meaning without Easter. The seven Sundays following Easter celebrate the joy of this event.

ASCENSION DAY: Falls forty days after Easter and celebrates Christ's ascension to heaven to be with the Father.

PENTECOST: Falls fifty days after Easter and considered to be the church's birthday. The day of Pentecost marks the beginning of the Pentecost season. This season spans a period of twenty-two to twenty-eight Sundays depending on the date on which Easter is celebrated. Pentecost emphasizes teaching about growth in the faith and life.

HOLY TRINITY SUNDAY: Celebrated on the first Sunday after the day of Pentecost and calls the church's attention to the Godhead, which is now complete as God the Father, God the Son, and God the Holy Spirit.

Each season or special day during the church year is denoted by a symbolic color.

WHITE: Festival of Christmas, Epiphany, Baptism of Jesus, Transfiguration, Easter, Holy Trinity, All Saints and Christ the King. White denotes purity, perfection, joy and the holiness of God.

PURPLE: Can be Advent, but Lent is more recognized by the color purple, which designates Jesus's humiliation and suffering for us. It is used during this season of preparation and penitence.

BLUE: Symbol of the Advent season. It denotes hope and expectation.

GREEN: Non- festival Sundays of Epiphany and the Pentecost season. It is the color of nature, abiding life, peace, nourishment, rest, constancy, and signifies Christian growth. It is used during the longer teaching seasons of the church year.

RED: Pentecost Sunday, Reformation Sunday, special festivals or rites, such as ordination. Red represents the saints of the church, the blood of martyrs, and the fire of the Spirit. It may also be used during Holy Week.

BLACK: Good Friday. The color denotes sadness and mourning.

Certain parts of the service, such as the Prayer of the Day, the lessons, and the gospel, reflect a specific theme of the church year. These parts are called *propers*. Each Sunday and special day has its own set of propers.

The Lutheran Church follows a three-year lectionary, as do as other Protestant churches and Roman Catholics. Matthew, Mark and Luke are the Gospel readings used by the church most often and are designated as Year A, Year B and Year C. The Gospel of John is dispersed throughout these three years.

Following the calendar for the church year, the lectionary contains complete texts of appointed Prayers of the Day, Psalms and lessons for each and every day, and is used by many during times of devotions.

NOTES

CHAPTER 10

The Basis and Heritage of Our Lutheran Worship Service

Observance of the Sabbath is fundamental to the life of Lutherans. The book of Exodus tells us that God blessed the Sabbath day and consecrated it. It is part of the original law given to Moses and the people. In the book of Deuteronomy, the command to observe the Sabbath is given by God in order for us to reflect upon the freeing, redeeming, and saving action of God, who has made us his people. The Sabbath is important, and God commanded us to observe it on a regular basis. Nowhere in Scripture does God make worship an option. At the same time however, nowhere does He give a formula for exactly how we should worship or what particular format we should use.

Lutheran worship is a visible expression of our faith. Worship ought to inform and inspire our practice and daily walk as Christians. Therefore, it is important for us to know what we are about as worshiping people and why we do what we do when we do it. Martin Luther, a Roman Catholic monk, was a pastoral reformer concerned with bad theology and practice, and how they impacted the lives of the worshiping community. If religion was viewed by the masses of people as little more than oppressive and burdensome superstition (which it was in Luther's day), then something was wrong. Basically, Luther felt that the Roman Catholic Church had taken Christ away from the people and in his place substituted just so much religious observance. Luther felt that this served to alienate the people from God. His work as a reformer in theology and practice always had about it an eye to restoring the people to a loving, living relationship with Jesus Christ.

To this end, Luther's most significant contribution was the translation of the Bible into the common language of the people (German). It was the first time Scripture had ever been translated into a common vernacular. Therefore, it was the first time that common men and women could read the Bible for themselves, meet the risen Christ in the pages of Holy Scripture and develop their own understanding and faith. Behind this was Luther's insistence on the priesthood of all believers. This was the idea that each and every man and woman understood they were their own priest and, therefore, able to go directly to God without the need of intermediaries to find pardon and strength.

Luther also brought worship into the language of the people so they could participate in the worship service rather than just observe it. To this end, he brought music and hymns back into the church as part of worship. More than any other Protestant church, Lutherans are known as a singing church. Thank Martin Luther for that; he wrote thirty-seven hymns, many of which he simply adapted from folk tunes and beer drinking songs. He made them hymns so that everyday people as peasants and farmers could participate in worship. Luther put people back in touch with Jesus Christ through the worship service. While our worship service today retains much from the old Roman Catholic Church, it is also profoundly influenced by the genius and pastoral concern of Martin Luther.

A bit of context when discussing Lutheran liturgical worship might be helpful. Perhaps you are familiar with the Biltmore house in Asheville, North Carolina. It's an inspiring mansion of 250 rooms built by George Vanderbilt who made (and inherited) his fortune in the transportation industry. Construction of the mansion and estate took six years and it was opened on Christmas Eve of 1895. If you've ever been there you know that to the right of the entrance hall is the indoor Winter Garden and to the right of that is the Banquet Hall a most impressive room measuring

72 feet long and 42 feet wide. It includes a 70-foot high barrel-vaulted ceiling, huge triple fireplace and in the center a massive table that seats thirty-two. Historians tell of the elaborate eight-course meals hosted by the Vanderbilt's on special occasions, guests dressed in their finest dining wear, Banquet Hall beautifully decorated, silver and crystal finery was set out with great care and the evening meal served with great pomp and elegance for the enjoyment of all. It must have been quite an experience – and, indeed, that was the intention!

That has relation to what we are doing in liturgical worship. Space and appointments and order are important! That's not to say that liturgical worship can't take place without it. However, the space and furnishings and order of things are important components of good liturgical worship because they serve to enhance the experience for all. That's why we build spaces constructed especially for worship with furnishings and appointments especially suited for worship. It's also why we do things in a specific and proper order. It's to enhance the experience of a meaningful encounter with God!

Lutherans understand that we worship because we are commanded by God to do so. We worship not with the idea that it is something we do for God, but rather because we are concerned about our relationship with God, and it is through worship that God is enabled to do something for us. Through the experience of worship our relationship with God is developed and deepened. Therefore, worship, like dinner at the Biltmore House, is a community experience of relationship with God and it lies at the very core of who we are.

Not to overdo the Biltmore thing, but it would be kind of odd to eat dinner alone at a table that seats thirty-two. Liturgical worship is a public affair, not a private one. It is something that is done together. For instance, at your baptism you are baptized into a community, a family, a body of believers. The service of Holy Baptism in the Lutheran Book of Worship states: "By water and the Holy Spirit we are made members of the Church which is the body of Christ. As we live with him <u>and with his people</u>, we grow in faith, love and obedience to the will of God." Liturgical worship is designed to be practiced together.

Beyond that, however, the directive of God is that worship should be a regular practice, not an occasional one. When it's time for dinner, you need to show up to be fed. What you do and where you are on Sunday morning is a signal and witness to your family, community and fellow church members what is important to you. A pattern of infrequent worship simply says, except for extenuating circumstances, that one's relationship with Jesus Christ is, at best, of secondary importance. Worship then is commanded by God, a public and corporate expression of faith done together, and ought to be reverenced with priority.

So, let's say that on a particular Sunday we made it to church. Good! Now, before the service starts, what we should do is begin to prepare ourselves for what is to come – an experience with God. This starts with the attitude we bring into the church. Great things can happen to and for us in worship, but we must be rightly prepared for it to happen. So upon coming into church, we should begin to re-focus our attention away from all that is out in the world: the neighbors, the dog, the boss, the power bill, or whatever the distraction might be. It is in worship that we come into contact, as incredible as it may seem, with an ancient power and the One who created this world and all that there is in it. In worship we are on holy ground. A sense of reverent awe ought to surround us as we begin to focus our attention away from the temporal to the things that are spiritual and unseen. Just as a craftsman or artist lays out tools before beginning a job or athletes warm up before the game, so at the beginning of our worship service we prepare our minds and hearts at the beginning of our worship service. Most Lutheran worship services have preservice music or a musical prelude, which sets the tone for the service. This preservice music is played not as conversation background - as these days in many churches it has become - but as invitation to solitude, reflection and preparation.

Following the prelude, there comes a time of self-examination is expressed in the Confession and Forgiveness. It's really a separate mini-service that prepares us for what is to come. This <u>corporate</u> Confession and Forgiveness (because our worship is practiced together) is made up of three parts: the Invocation, the Public Confession, and the Absolution.

The words of the Invocation, "In the name of the Father, and of the Son, and of the Holy Spirit" stand as a notice at the beginning of the service toward whom our attention and service is directed. We invoke or call on the name of the triune God in whose name we have been baptized, asking that he be present with us and bring us his blessing and instruction. The congregation responds with the ancient declaration of "amen," which is one of the oldest and most powerful words in the liturgy. The word amen literally means *this is absolutely true.* At the same time, it has behind its meaning the character of an oath. Therefore, saying amen is an affirmation not only of something's worth, but also of the fact that you agree with and affirm it.

The Public Confession of Sins follows the Invocation. Sometimes Lutherans get flack about this because what we are doing is reminding ourselves we are not the best and that we have fallen short of what God would intend. The reason for this is the fact that the Bible tells us that the barrier lying between God and ourselves is the barrier of sin, and we must take this very seriously. God did! God took sin so seriously that He sent his Son Jesus Christ to die on a cross on account of it.

The Invocation and Public Confession of Sin stand front and center at the beginning of the worship service. It means that we are admitting our need for God because we are not and have not been all that we should be. When we stand naked in the light of God's judgment, we are found to be lacking. We might as well be honest before God because there is nothing we can hide from him. So in public and corporate confession, we remove our mask of self-righteousness and admit before God and one another that we have missed the mark God intended for us. We ask God that we not be deceived into thinking that we have no need of forgiveness. And then, as the confession in the old Service Book and Hymnal states, "we flee for refuge to thine infinite mercy, seeking and imploring thy grace." We ask that God grants us, by his grace, the power to live more like the sons and daughters he made us to be.

As we confess together the reality of our sin, we are then presented the remedy of the cross through absolution. Absolution shifts the focus from the inadequacy of ourselves to the adequacy of God as we hear again God's promise and declaration of forgiveness. The pastor speaks in the place of God to the congregation: "In the mercy of almighty God, Jesus Christ was given to die for you and for his sake God forgives you all your sins." In this little rite of preparation, the timeless epic of God's salvation history is played out. Again and again, we are rescued from the slavery of sin as the children of Israel were rescued from their slavery in Egypt. No longer are we slaves of sin, but a free people through God's forgiveness. It is in this mood of freedom, enthusiasm and celebration that worship continues - or at least it should.

Some people think Lutheran worship is a somber and serious experience, but it is only because Lutherans seem to make it that way. Curiously, many Lutherans for whatever reason, don't understand that liturgical worship is not intended to be such. Yes, our worship service is orderly, but it is an orderly, joyous expression that is all about what God in Christ has accomplished for us through the cross.

The service proper has three main sections. The Entrance Rite, the Proclamation of the Word and the Celebration of the Eucharist. The Entrance Rite begins with the Apostolic Greeting. It is both a blessing and a greeting taken from the Apostle Paul's greeting to the church in II Corinthians 13:14. The words speak for themselves, namely our identity around God's name brings us to grace, love, and fellowship which is something as God's people we are privileged to share. It is used at the beginning of the service to remind us of the long tradition of faith and worship in which we stand.

After the pastor has spoken the Greeting, we come to what is really a sung prayer called the Kyrie or Kyrie eleison. The word Kyrie comes from the Greek word for lord and is often used in the phrase Kyrie eleison or Lord have mercy. This phrase is used as a response to the various petitions within this sung prayer, which focus is on the themes of peace, salvation, a prevailing sense of unity within the church of Christ and God's blessing upon the gathered people of God. It is a prayer for God's mercy so that his peace would reign in the church, our lives, and the world.

After the Kyrie comes the Hymn of Praise. It recalls the song of the angels as they announced the birth of Christ, "Glory to God in the highest . . ." and is sung as a hymn of celebration that tells of God's intervention in human history through his Son. This is the reason for our celebration as it is a fitting response to him who takes away the sin of the world. The Hymn of Praise is, in part, a biblical song from the book of Revelation which reminds us of Christ's death and resurrection, and of a future heavenly banquet that all God's saints will one day share together. Due to the more penitential tone of worship during the season of Lent, the Hymn of Praise is generally omitted.

Following the Hymn of Praise is the Prayer of the Day. This prayer has its origins in the ancient Collect which comes from the collected prayers of the people. Traditionally, parishioners would hand the pastor specific prayer requests on slips of paper as they entered the church in days gone by. The pastor would collect them and offer prayers for them at the altar at a point in the service. This tradition of collecting the prayers has moved in our modern service to the place in the service referred to as the Prayers of the Church or Prayers of Intercession. The Prayer of the Day is now used to tie together the theme of worship for that particular Sunday of the church year.

Next comes the second main portion of the service, the Proclamation of the Word. Each Sunday of the church year has a designation with appointed readings or lessons. The first lesson/reading is from the Old Testament, except during the weeks of Easter, when they are from the book of the Acts of the Apostles. When the Old Testament lessons are appointed, they usually come from the Torah (the first five books of the Bible), one of the books of the prophets, or from the one of the books of wisdom. Normally, the Old Testament lesson deals with the covenant God made with his people, the wisdom he showed to his people, or some important point in the history of Israel.

Having heard the first reading/lesson, the congregation responds with a Psalmody taken from the book of Psalms. Psalms were often used as hymns or liturgies in the early church and are used here as a reflection on the Old Testament reading. It reminds us of how the Word of God was integrated into the minds of God's people in ancient times. Next comes the second reading/lesson, which used to be referred to as the Epistle Lesson. The word epistle comes from the Greek and means letter. The books of the Bible from which these readings are taken were actually letters written by the great leaders of the early church giving instruction or dealing with certain issues that arose in the congregations. When leaders of early Christian communities received these letters, they were read to the entire congregation. New Christians were eager to hear what was going on within other communities that followed Jesus and hear instruction from authoritative leaders of the church. One fairly unique part of liturgical worship is that Scriptures are read unfiltered. We gather today just as Christians did 2000 years ago to hear with our own ears about the faith, insight, and instruction expressed by the original authors of the Bible.

Between the reading of the Epistle and the reading of the Gospel, there is a sung verse from Scripture to signify a transition that used to be known as the Gradual. The term Gradual stems from the Latin term meaning step or on the steps. With the use of lay readers in today's worship services, this brief portion of the service is now known as the Verse or Gospel Acclamation. It is simply a transition to the reading of the Gospel. Years ago, this Verse was sung as the pastor stepped from the lectern and up the steps of the pulpit in a reverent manner in order to show the importance or precedence of the Gospel. At this point in the service, the congregation stands in preparation of hearing God's word as proclaimed in the holy gospel. In the reading of the Gospel, Christ comes to us anew in our day and time. For that reason, the Gospel should be read by the presiding minister who functions to represent Christ in the midst of his people. The Gospel Acclamation ends with the sung Alleluia, which literally means praise the Lord. It is an ancient chant of joy and praise sung as the congregation prepares to hear the words of Christ spoken among us today.

The great fourth century theologian Augustine said, "Let us listen to the Gospel as if the Lord himself stood before us." So, we stand prior to the reading of the gospel out of respect to welcome Christ into our midst.

A high point of the worship service is reached with the proclamation of the Word in the reading of the Gospel. As the Gospel is announced, the congregation stands and responds, "Glory to you, O Lord," which shows the honor and reverence deserved by the reading of these words. The Gospel gives us insight as to the actions, conversations, and teachings of our Lord. We hear of and thereby share in his sufferings, death and resurrection very much as a person might share in all the emotion of a story or family letter being read. Hearing the words, we receive assurance that Christ is our savior, our victor over sin, and by God's grace, we have salvation and are restored to newness of life. Following the reading of the Gospel, we respond with "Praise to you, O Christ." These are words of thanksgiving for the word of salvation accomplished for us in the life, death, resurrection and ascension of our Lord to which we have just been witness.

Next comes the Sermon. It is important to understand the purpose of a sermon. A sermon is to expound, clarify, and bring home the Word of God. A sermon is not twenty minutes of pulpit pounding, entertainment, or pleasing oratory. Rather, a sermon should seek to address two issues. First, it serves to proclaim and lift up Jesus. As Paul wrote to the Corinthian church, "But we preach Christ crucified." Our focus is to proclaim what has been done for us through the life, death and resurrection of our Lord. This is the "Good News," and it just may be the only good news some have heard all week! Second, what does Jesus' teaching mean for our daily lives and how are we to respond in the way that we live?

The last major division of the service centers on our response to God's word in what has come before. This portion of the service often includes Holy Communion, but sometimes not. This section begins with the Hymn of the Day which is generally selected to tie in with the theme of the lessons for the particular Sunday and the sermon.

Next comes the confession of the Creed. Having received God's forgiveness and been strengthened by His word, we now state what we believe as the church through one of two creeds: the Apostles' Creed and the Nicene Creed. These are recited alternatively depending on the Sunday and season of the church year. These creeds are the major confessional expressions of our faith. The creeds, however, do not necessarily express an individual's faith because that may differ from one person to another. The creeds are meant to express the faith of the church which the people of God affirm together.

The Apostles' Creed comes from the old Roman Creed which was used in the context of baptism. It is a concise and straightforward affirmation of the faith of the church going back to the apostles. The Nicene Creed was developed by the Council of Nicea in 325. Its purpose was to give fuller expression to the faith of the church and also to combat what was known at that time as the Arian heresy or Arian controversy, which raged over opposing views about God. One group, headed by Bishop Alexander of Alexandria, proclaimed that there were three persons in one God. Others, headed by Eusebius and Arius, a presbyter in Alexandria, believed in only one indivisible God.

The service continues with the Prayers of Intercession, which are based on the promises and greatness of God. We offer our prayers with an attitude of confidence that God wills our good and has the power to grant it. In the prayers we pray for the church, the world, and all in need. It is a time to bring our concerns to God not only as individuals, but as a congregation. The prayers lift up the needs of the community, the world, and the congregation, and call us to action as we leave worship having been strengthened, fortified, and uplifted do God's will in the world. When Holy Communion is not celebrated, the Offering follows Creed, followed by the prayers, which includes the Lord's Prayer.

In most Lutheran congregations what follows is the Sharing of the Peace. One Lutheran Church publication in its welcome brochure talking about the worship service and the Sharing of the Peace said: "this is when all hell breaks loose!" It can seem that way, but it is certainly not the intention.

If and when the Sharing of the Peace becomes a period of time for "chit-chat" and conviviality, there is a problem. After the prayers, the pastor says, "The peace of the Lord be with you always," to which the congregation responds, "And also with you." Having the peace that comes from God, the congregation is now instructed to reconcile with each other before taking communion together.

The Table of the Lord is not a meal eaten among enemies, but among family and friends. Because of this, the passing of the peace is not a nicety or passive moment, but a bold act of declaring our reconciliation as children of God. Sometimes this is not easy. Healing wounds, hurts, and broken relationships is a difficult task, but it was the task of the cross. Each time we make peace with each other, we point to that triumph of God's love through the cross. We share the peace (and not an update on our lower back pain) in affirmation that not only have we been reconciled to God, we have been reconciled to each other.

Next follows the Offering. Here we should be motivated to give back to God a portion of the blessings we receive from him. These blessings include our time, talents, and financial resources. Giving to the Lord through the church should bring us joy in knowing that we are supporting the work of the church, both at home and abroad As we offer these gifts up to the altar, we symbolize offering ourselves as living sacrifices and the offering becomes a visual expression and example of our promise to be servants of God for his church and one another.

Now we are almost ready to eat! The celebration of the Eucharist (from the Greek, meaning thanksgiving) begins with The Great Thanksgiving. This is a simple dialog, sung or recited that Christians have used for centuries as they prepare to receive the Lord's Supper. The Proper Preface follows, which is a prayer thanking God for the blessing we receive through Christ and a reminder of what is to come. The Preface is PROPER for that particular Sunday's theme or season of the church year.

Next comes the Sanctus, from the Latin and means holy. It is a normally sung expression of praise for the Holy One who is once again among his people to give of himself in bread and wine. The words holy, holy, holy in the Sanctus reminds us of Isaiah's vision in the temple (Isaiah 6) and of the chants of welcome when Jesus entered Jerusalem on Palm Sunday.

Following the Sanctus, in the Words of Institution we hear of the Last Supper and remember Jesus gathering with his disciples to share this meal of remembrance and redemption. We hear the gracious invitation to receive the very life of the one who was offered on the cross for our sins. To conclude our thanksgiving, we pray the Lord's Prayer that Jesus taught his disciples. In effect, the Lord's Prayer becomes the congregation's table prayer before receiving this life-giving offering of body and blood.

After the Lord's Prayer the Agnus Dei or Lamb of God canticle is sung. It reminds us of the words spoken by John at Jesus' baptism, "Behold, the Lamb of God, who takes away the sins of the world." (John 1:29) It also reminds us of the connection between Passover and Easter. When the children of Israel were delivered from their slavery in Egypt, Moses told the people to kill an unblemished lamb and put its blood on the doorpost of their homes. The angel of death that God sent as the last plague on Egypt PASSED OVER these homes so marked and the people were spared. Remembering this deliverance from slavery in Egypt, the Jews celebrated the Passover every year. As the disciples were Jews, after the crucifixion it was easy for them to make the connection of Jesus as the Lamb of God, who was sacrificed that people might be delivered from their bondage to sin and death.

Following the distribution of the sacrament, the congregation may sing a Post Communion Canticle. This is a true expression of joyous gratitude for the gift of life we have here and in the world to come. The Post Communion Canticle and the Closing Prayer connect what the Lord has done for us in the future world with what we are to do for him in the present one. Our worship is to be carried on in our daily lives. We are to conform our lives to his. We are to tell everyone what he has done.

Finally, the Benediction or Blessing" (Numbers 6:22-27) is pronounced, which is the Aaronic Blessing that was first used by the church in the

11th century. The sign of the cross can be made by all at this point in the service as a reminder of Christ in whose name we are baptized. So then, we depart worship with a blessing on our heads and willingness in our hearts to share the good news of Jesus Christ in word and deed. What a fine experience it has been!

Such is the heritage of the Lutheran Church and such is our worship.

NOTES

_____

_____

_____

_____

_____

_____

_____

_____

_____

_____

_____

_____

_____

_____

_____

_____

_____

_____

_____

_____

_____

_____

_____

_____

_____

_____

_____

CHAPTER **11**

The Faith of the Church —
The Apostles' Creed

Most Sunday mornings, Lutheran congregations will confess together the Apostles' Creed. The Apostles' Creed is a confession or declaration of the apostolic Christian faith, not because it was written by the Apostles (it was not), but because it expresses the teaching of the apostles regarding the Christian faith. An apostle is defined as one who has seen the risen Christ or one who is sent with a specific mission. The Apostles' Creed was fixed in its final form by the Roman Catholic Church in the late sixth century.

Historically, creeds served three main purposes: 1) to set forth the belief of the Christian community or WITNESS; 2) to draw the line between accepted and rejected belief or BOUNDARY; AND 3) as a summary for teaching the faith to converts or INSTRUCTION.

Today, the Apostles' Creed serves these same functions. However, it is important to remember, especially for those new to the church or Christian faith, that confessing the faith of the church and confessing one's individual faith are not necessarily one in the same. To be sure, the Apostles' Creed may be an accurate expression of one's faith (or for new Christians it may not be), but the creed is not used as a confession that one must adhere to in order to be admitted into church membership. Rather, the Apostles' Creed expresses the faith of the Christian church and, therefore, the faith that will be taught, preached, and revered within this Christian community. The question that is asked upon joining the church is not whether one believes in the Apostles' Creed, but rather do you want to belong to a community that does?

Remember that liturgical worship is based upon the idea of community. There is no such thing as an individual worship consciousness. We are related to God in the context of worship as a family. We share together the responsibility for our sinfulness, God's forgiveness, and His blessings. As we confess the creed in worship, it is not an individual faith we profess, but the faith of the people of God, the family, the body of Christ.

I BELIEVE

These first words of the creed would seem to fly in the face of what was just said above. However, the sense here is that, as a member of Christ's church, the expression of faith in the Apostles' Creed is part of one's responsibility. Remember the purposes of the creed is witness, boundary, and instruction. The expression "I believe" indicates that one has a responsibility for the faith of the church in that it is the faith their church confesses. When one says, "I believe" at the beginning of the creed, in effect they are saying they stand with those who will do their best to honor, proclaim and teach this set of beliefs regarding God, Jesus Christ and the Holy Spirit.

By the way, the Apostles' Creed (hereafter AP) is a Trinitarian formulation. Its three articles indicate what we believe about God, what we believe about Jesus Christ, and what we believe about the Holy Spirit.

Note that belief is not exact or verifiable information, but a confession of certainty by which a man or a woman lives. They order their lives by these certainties even though they may not be proved. For example, a wife plans dinner to be ready at 6 p.m. because she believes that her husband will come home from work to eat at that time, not be on a boat to Tahiti to "find himself." Belief is not something that can necessarily be proved, but it is not doubted. If someone believes that people are basically bad and everyone is out to get them, they tend to live their lives angry and guarded ways. If, on the other hand, one believes that people are basically good and that they can be trusted and relied upon, they will live their lives in more trusting and content ways. Neither premise can be proved, but neither is doubted. It is upon the certainty of one's beliefs that they order their lives.

ARTICLE ONE

I BELIEVE IN GOD THE FATHER ALMIGHTY

Here we confess that we believe that there is someone behind our existence. We affirm that our being is not the result of some chance series of events, but rather of an intentional, creative personality. Humanity and the world didn't just happen via cosmic chaos over billions of years. However our being came about, we confess that it was by the action and resolve of an intentional, deliberate, designed, creative plan of God.

MAKER OF HEAVEN AND EARTH

This phrase continues the thought expressed above that God is the author of all life, all existence and all things. God is creator and has set order and logic into his creation extending from his greatest work, which is the human being in His own image, down to the smallest one-cell organism. God has not only planned all existence, he carried that plan out made it and continues his creative process in and through us.

The main thrust of the first article of the Apostles' Creed, however, is to posit a creative personhood behind our existence. As this personhood, e.g. God, continues to be active in his creation, he continues to care for it and for us.

ARTICLE TWO

I BELIEVE IN JESUS CHRIST, HIS ONLY SON OUR LORD

The main intent here is *who* Jesus Christ was. If we accept the idea of God from Article One, then the message or Word from God has come to us in the man Jesus. The creed affirms that Jesus Christ not only revealed God, he was God in the incarnated human form of his Son. The message and teaching of Jesus loses much of its weight apart from the affirmation of who he was. In professing the identity of Jesus, the church affirms that following Jesus is following God.

CONCEIVED BY THE HOLY GHOST, BORN OF THE VIRGIN MARY

In this section of the creed, we may come to the difficulty in accepting the possibility of a virgin birth. This author personally has little trouble with this possibility because I think God is not bound by our limitations. Indeed, I think the creation of a baby in the normal way is a greater miracle than impregnation in an extraordinary way. But that aside, we must not think that the phrase "born of the virgin Mary" is trying to get us to accept something about the state of Mary's reproductive system at the time of conception. This is not about biology—it is about identity.

The theological truth and intent of this phrase is to affirm Jesus as totally unique, unlike anyone else who has been or will be. This Jesus of Nazareth was holy other - the incarnation (or the being made into human flesh) of God Himself.

Note that in the Bible, Jesus never refers to or touts his virgin birth. It is never used it as a test for the faith of a believer. People came to believe in Jesus Christ through their encounters with him. It is still true today. As we come into contact with the living Christ through the church, Scripture, and the sacraments, we grow into a faith which affirms Jesus as God's only begotten Son. Therefore, the virgin birth is not something we necessarily accept about Jesus. Rather it is something we affirm as we grow in faith to know Jesus Christ as one unlike any other.

SUFFERED UNDER PONTIUS PILATE

The key word here is *suffered*. We affirm that Jesus was truly God, but also truly human. His divinity did not preclude him from experiencing life fully human. Jesus felt, acted, and experienced life as a human being. Therefore, he knew what it was like to be like on of us. Our God knows the human condition, and what it's like to be down here because he has been here to experience it. He knows of human tragedy and triumph, sorrow and joy, and all the emotions and experiences that make up life and living.

The suffering at the hands of Pilate is an important affirmation for the church because of this witness to Jesus' humanity. Our prayers are offered to and heard by a God who knows our trials and temptations by experience. Jesus' passion indicates the great a love he showed for us in undergoing the agony of the cross, but the relational aspect is also powerful. We can relate to God in Jesus Christ because he has already related to us. We have a common bond in our sharing of humanity.

WAS CRUCIFIED, DIED AND WAS BURIED

This is the oldest Christian kerygma (teaching) contained within the creed. The central facts regarding Jesus had to do with his death, burial, rising, and appearing. (Paul emphasizes these same things in 1 Corinthians 15: 3-8.) The definitive words here, however, are about Jesus' literal death confirmed by the fact that he was buried. This is an important affirmation of the creed that Christ truly died if the resurrection is to hold any meaning. The resurrection is not to be understood as resuscitation, but an actual victory over the power of death.

HE DESCENDED INTO HELL

The intent of this phrase can be lost if we think of hell in spatial terms. The emphasis is more on the condition caused by death. In fact, some versions of the Apostles' Creed substitute the word death for hell. It is an option in newer Lutheran liturgical books. The point is that death separates one from God and God's love. Theologically speaking, it is the absence of God that is hell. Apart from God's love and mercy, there is no hope, no forgiveness, no love, nothing, and that, therefore, is hell. The focus could be on hell as a place of punishment, but then Jesus required no punishment in that he was sinless. Therefore, the more helpful reading is that, in dying, Jesus faced what we all face: isolation and separation from the power of God's love. This is the awful power of death. That is hell.

ON THE THIRD DAY HE ROSE AGAIN FROM THE DEAD

This phrase brings us to the central proclamation of the Christian faith that, by the power of God, Jesus Christ was raised from the dead. This action of God broke through the prior impenetrable barrier imposed by death. This was a new revelation or new work of God through his Son. A way to eternal salvation created in the flashpoint between Christ's suffering and God's love.

ASCENDED INTO HEAVEN AND IS SEATED ON THE RIGHT HAND OF GOD THE FATHER ALMIGHTY

Here again we can lose the intent of this phrase by thinking of heaven in spatial terms. The theological affirmation is that Jesus was given a place of authority in God's rule, reign, or dominion which is not limited by time or space. The right hand is symbolic of power or authority, and so the intent of this phrase is that Jesus has a place of authority in God's kingdom. Much of Jesus' teaching was based on his relationship with the Father, as was much of what he promised for us eternally. This relationship between the Father and the Son, wherein the judgment of Jesus becomes the judgment of God, is affirmed here.

It is also the affirmation of the creed that Jesus was bodily carried into heaven or ascended in the flesh. The New Testament image of Christ as a man and at the same time being divine is preserved here. Christ's nature is never divided so that one might think that his body returned to dust, but Jesus still lives in his spirit. Our image of Jesus is consistently that of a true man and true God at the same time. When we say Christ is present in the Holy Communion, this is not a spiritual presence but a physical presence when we receive into our hands and mouths his true body and blood.

FROM WHERE HE SHALL COME TO JUDGE THE LIVING AND THE DEAD

This follows naturally in that, from Jesus' position of power and authority in God's reign, he is able to grant eternal life. Jesus said, "I am the way and the truth and the life. No one comes to the Father but by me." (John 14:6) Jesus, in this affirmation of the creed, is seen as not only our savior, but our advocate before the judgment of God as well. Jesus has promised us eternal life. In God's kingdom he has the power and authority to do so.

<u>ARTICLE THREE</u>

I BELIEVE IN THE HOLY SPIRIT

The Holy Spirit is the personal influence of God that is among us today. Through the church in its proclamation of the Word and administration of the sacraments, the Holy Spirit works to bring us to faith and holy living. In the time of Christ, the breath was seen as the life of the body. Sometimes, upon the death of someone, we say that person has expired, or the breath has gone out of them. The Greek for the word spirit, pneuma, is translated wind or breath. Therefore, the Spirit is that which brings life. We define the church as the Body of Christ, and therefore would say that it is the Holy Spirit that gives life to the body of Christ, the church.

In affirming the Holy Spirit, the creed professes the power of Christ - the power of the Gospel - to breathe new life into human hearts. It professes the Word that is able to come alive within us and become a creative, transforming power in our life. Words have power when they are linked to some meaning or purpose in our lives. The Holy Spirit links the words of God contained in Scripture to our lives in such a way that we are transformed to live life differently, e.g. more like the people God would have us be.

I BELIEVE IN THE HOLY catholic CHURCH, THE COMMUNION OF SAINTS

There are two uses of the word catholic. Catholic with a capital C indicates the Roman Catholic Church. Catholic with a lower case c means universal. This portion of the creed, therefore, affirms a broad expression of the church. The true church is not the Lutheran Church, the Baptist Church, the Episcopal Church, the Catholic Church, the Methodist Church, or any other. Rather, the true church exists universally wherever and whenever people are joined to Jesus Christ through water (baptism) and the Word (the gospel). A saint (lower case) is differentiated from a Saint (capitalized) in that it refers not to a marvelous Christian, but rather a forgiven sinner. Therefore, the communion of saints is the gathering of those sinners who have been forgiven in Christ who make up the church. Therefore, this is a broad expression of the church; those who are joined to Christ through faith, not by denomination.

THE FORGIVENESS OF SINS

Paul said "the wages of sin is death" (Romans 6:23) and the Christian faith affirms that sin brings separation from God. By God's love and mercy, the repentant are granted forgiveness and thereby acceptability before God. It is because of forgiveness that we have standing before God. This freedom from guilt enables us to have life now. This freedom from penalty enables us to have life everlasting.

THE RESURRECTION OF THE BODY AND THE LIFE EVERLASTING

The creed affirms the Christian hope of eternal life based upon Christ's resurrection and the forgiveness of sins. The final enemy that would seek to separate us from God is vanquished by Christ's resurrection and by his authority in God's kingdom, we are made heirs to an eternal home with the Father. The idea of bodily resurrection also affirms the concept of the resurrection of the <u>personality</u>. Paul said that we would be embodied in heaven not with flesh and blood, but with spiritual bodies. We are not sure what that means exactly and neither was Paul, but we trust enough to leave it up to God. The affirmation, however, is that who we are (our personhood), will not be lost as we cross over to the other side. We will know our loved ones in heaven and they will know us.

NOTES

"*Unless I am convinced by the testimony of the Scriptures and by clear reason (for I do not trust in the pope or councils alone, since it is well known that they have often erred and contradicted themselves), I am bound by the Scriptures I have quoted. My conscience is captive to the Word of God. I cannot and I will not retract anything, since it is neither safe nor right to go against conscience. May God help me. Amen.*"

Martin Luther

NOTES

1   Eric W. Gritsch, and Robert W. Jenson: *Lutheranism: The Theological Movement and Its Confessional Writings* (Philadelphia: Fortress Press, 1976), 166.

2   Paul Althaus: *The Theology of Martin Luther.* trans. Robert C. Schultz (Philadelphia; Fortress Press, 1981), 341.

3   Ibid. 345.

4   Fredrick Buechner: *Wishful Thinking: A Seekers ABC* (San Francisco: HarperSanFrancisco, 1993), 101.

5   Timothy J. Wengert, edited by Jeffrey S. Nelson and Elizabeth Drotning. *Luther's Small Catechism.* (Minneapolis: Augsburg Fortress, 2001), 47.

6   Fredrick Buechner: *Wishful Thinking: A Seekers ABC* (San Francisco: HarperSanFrancisco, 1993), 6.

7   Ibid. 6.

8   Timothy J. Wengert, edited by Jeffrey S. Nelson and Elizabeth Drotning. *Luther's Small Catechism.* (Minneapolis: Augsburg Fortress, 2001), 57.

9   Fredrick Buechner: *Wishful Thinking: A Seekers ABC* (San Francisco: HarperSanFrancisco, 1993), 63.

10 Ibid. 38-39.

11 Timothy J. Wengert, edited by Jeffrey S. Nelson and Elizabeth Drotning. *Luther's Small Catechism.* (Minneapolis: Augsburg Fortress, 2001),57.

Use of Clip Art: Permission granted by Copyright Specialist Content Management, 1517 Media, 510 Marquette Ave. 8th Floor, Minneapolis MN 55402 Augsburg Fortress, Fortress Press Sparkhouse.

Scripture quotations are from the Revised Standard Version of the Bible, copyright © 1946, 1952, and 1971 the Division of Christian Education of the National Council of the Churches of Christ in the United States of America. Used by permission. All rights reserved.

Postscript: Surely over the last 35 years of ordained ministry, teaching, preaching studying, and collecting material, we may have unconsciously borrowed from others. If so, our gratitude and apologies to all!

BIBLIOGRAPHY

Althaus, Paul, *The Theology of Martin Luther.* trans. Robert C. Schultz, Philadelphia: Fortress Press, 1981.

Aulen, Gustaf, Translated by Eric Wahlstrom, *The Faith of the Christian Church.* Philadelphia: Fortress Press, 1960.

Benson, Kathleen, *A Man Called Martin Luther.* St. Louis: Concordia Publishing House. 1980.

Buechner, Fredrick, *Wishful Thinking: A Seekers ABC.* San Francisco: HarperSanFrancisco, 1993.

Deitz, Reginald, *Luther and the Reformation.* Philadelphia: Fortress Press, 1953.

Fischer, Robert, *Luther.* Philadelphia: Lutheran Church Press, 1966

Fredriksen, Paula, *From Jesus to Christ: The Origins of the New Testament Images of Jesus.* Binghamton, N.Y.: Vail-Ballou Press, 1988.

Gritsch, Eric W. and Robert W. Jenson, *Lutheranism: The Theological Movement and Its Confessional Writing.* Philadelphia: Fortress Press, 1976.

Klos, Frank, (With Articles of Lasting Interest By George F. Hall and Others), *Being In The Body Of Christ.* Philadelphia: Fortress Press, 1975.

Luther's Works, Volume 31.

Janzow, Samuel F, *Luther's Large Catechism*: *Contemporary Translation*. St. Louis: Concordia Publishing House, 1978.

Wegener, Mark I., *Rituals of Redemption. Sermons on the Meaning of Liturgical Ceremonies*. Lima: Fairway Press, 1992.

Wengert, Timothy J., edited by Jeffrey S. Nelson and Elizabeth Drotning, *Luther's Small Catechism*. Minneapolis: Augsburg Fortress, 2001.

Being Lutheran Today: A Layperson's Guide to Our History, Belief and Practice will help the reader understand what Lutherans believe about the basics of the Christian faith. In easy to read language, you are given a historical perspective of the core beliefs of those who count themselves as Lutherans. The book sets forth the tenets of Lutheran doctrine; what Lutherans generally believe in practice; how to read the Bible; what the sacraments of baptism and Holy Communion are about for Lutherans; the basics of Lutheran worship and the faith of the church expressed in the Apostles' Creed.

This book is a very helpful resource for those congregations seeking to reach out to previously un-churched members or transfer members from different denominations....The easy to read format and easy to understand writing style of this book makes it particularly enjoyable to read and share with others. It begins by giving the reader a history of the subject, and each successive chapter digs deeper into the faith practices of Lutherans, allowing the reader to develop a thorough understanding of the material. I encourage Christian education leaders, pastors, and anyone wanting to understand who we are as a denomination to read this fantastic book and learn about our heritage and practices as Lutherans.

❖ From the Forward by The Rev. Patti Sue Burton-Pye
   Providence Lutheran Church, Lexington, South Carolina

This is an outstanding resource for teaching adults Lutheran beliefs especially those who are contemplating joining a Lutheran congregation. It would also be an excellent resource for adult confirmation instruction.

❖ James S. Aull, PhD
   Bishop of the South Carolina Synod, Retired

As someone entering the Lay Ministry who has not attended seminary, *Being Lutheran Today: A Layperson's Guide to our History, Belief and Practice,* is an invaluable resource. It offers history of Lutherans and Lutheranism, a brief theology, tips on how to read the Bible, Sacraments, Creeds, describes worship, and my favorite section which is on church seasons and colors. For someone new to Lutheranism, dating or marrying a Lutheran, wants to know more about Lutherans, or just wants a quick reference, this is the book for you. It is like the Cliff Notes of Lutheranism!

❖ Laura Sharp-Waites, Ed.D., Deaconess Student

Printed in the United States
By Bookmasters